Praise for *The Populist Explosion*

"*The Populist Explosion* is far and away the most incisive examination of the central development in contemporary politics: the rise of populism on both the right and the left. John Judis, whose track record is unrivaled, is the ideal author to tackle the subject, and he has done a superb job, placing contemporary trends, including the rise of Donald Trump, in historical perspective. Judis demonstrates the crucial role of the 2008 recession both here and in Europe in discrediting the neoliberal agenda. This is must reading."

—**Thomas Edsall,**
New York Times columnist

"*The Populist Explosion* blends groundbreaking reporting with insightful scholarship in the best guide yet to the most important political phenomenon of our time."

—**Michael Lind,**
author of *Land of Promise:*
An Economic History of the United States

"John Judis demonstrates again why he is one of America's best political journalists. There is no wiser or better informed analysis of contemporary voter discontent on both sides of the Atlantic than *The Populist Explosion*."

—**Michael Kazin,**
editor of *Dissent*, author of *The Populist Persuasion:*
An American History and *War Against War:*
The American Fight for Peace, 1914-1918

The Populist Explosion

How the Great Recession Transformed American and European Politics

COLUMBIA GLOBAL REPORTS
NEW YORK

The Populist Explosion

How the Great Recession Transformed American and European Politics

John B. Judis

United
States

Published by Columbia Global Reports
91 Claremont Avenue, Suite 515
New York, NY 10027
globalreports.columbia.edu
facebook.com/columbiaglobalreports
@columbiaGR

Library of Congress Control Number: 2016945882
ISBN: 978-0997126440

Book design by Charlotte Strick and Claire Williams
Map design by Jeffrey L. Ward
Author photograph by Hilary P. Judis

Printed in the United States of America

For Jon Cohn, Richard Just, and Josh Marshall

CONTENTS

What Is Populism, and Why Is It Important?

Populist parties and candidates are on the move in the United States and Europe. Donald Trump has won the Republican nomination; Bernie Sanders came in a very strong second to Hillary Clinton for the Democratic nomination. And these candidacies came on the heels of the Tea Party and Occupy Wall Street movements. In Europe, populist parties in France, Sweden, Norway, Finland, Denmark, Austria, Greece, Italy, Spain, and Switzerland are contending for power or are already part of the government.

In France, the National Front (FN) came in first in the regional elections in December 2015 with 27.73 percent of the vote, but was denied a victory in the regional presidencies because the Republican and Socialist parties joined forces against it in the runoff. In Denmark, the People's Party (DF) came in second in the June 2015 parliamentary elections. In Austria, Freedom Party (FPÖ) candidate Norbert Hofer came in first in the first round of the presidential election in April 2016.

In Switzerland, the Swiss People's Party (SVP) came in first in the parliamentary elections with 29.4 percent of the vote,

almost twice the total of the Social Democrats and the Liberals. In Norway, the Progress Party (FrP) has been part of the
ruling government coalition since 2013. In the Netherlands,
Geert Wilders's Freedom Party (PVV), currently the country's
third largest party, is well ahead in polls for the 2017 parliamentary elections. Britain's United Kingdom Independence Party
(UKIP), after disappointing results in the 2015 parliamentary
elections, bounced back in local elections, ousting the Labour
Party in Wales and was at the forefront of the British campaign
to exit the European Union.

In Europe, populist parties have also arisen on the left and
center-left. In Italy, comedian Beppe Grillo's Five Star Movement
won the most seats in the 2013 election to the Chamber of Dep-
uties. In the June 2016 municipal elections, Five Star candidate
Virginia Raggi was elected Rome's mayor with 67 percent of the
vote. In Spain, the Podemos Party, founded in 2014, came in third
in the December 2015 and June 2016 parliamentary elections. In
Greece, the decade-old Syriza Party came in first in two parliamentary elections in 2015, and took charge of the government.
This book is about how these populist candidates and movements have come about, and why in the wake of the Great Recession, they have proven so successful in mobilizing support.

Defining Populism

When political scientists write about populism, they often begin
by trying to define it, as if it were a scientific term like entropy
or photosynthesis. That's a mistake. There is no set of features
that exclusively defines movements, parties, and people that are
called populist—from the Russian Narodniks to Huey Long, and
from France's Marine Le Pen to the late congressman Jack Kemp.
As with ordinary language, even more so with ordinary *political*
language, the different people and parties called "populist" enjoy

14   family resemblances of one to the other, but not a set of traits can be found exclusively in all of them.

There is, however, a kind of populist politics that originated in the United States in the nineteenth century, has recurred in the twentieth and twenty-first centuries, and in the 1970s began to appear in Western Europe. Whereas populist parties and movements in Latin America have sometimes tried to subvert the democratic competition for power, the populist campaigns and parties in the United States and Western Europe have embraced it. In the last decades, these campaigns and parties have converged in their concerns, and in the wake of the Great Recession, they have surged. That's the subject of this book: I want to say a little about what this kind of populist politics is, and why it includes both Trump and Sanders and both France's National Front and Spain's Podemos.

First of all, the kind of populism that runs through American history, and is transplanted to Europe, cannot be defined in terms of right, left, or center. There are rightwing, leftwing and centrist populist parties. It is not an ideology, but a political logic—a way of thinking about politics. In his book on American populism, *The Populist Persuasion*, historian Michael Kazin gets part of this logic. Populism, he writes, is "a language whose speakers conceive of ordinary people as a noble assemblage not bounded narrowly by class; view their elite opponents as self-serving and undemocratic; and seek to mobilize the former against the latter."

That's a good start. It doesn't describe someone like Ronald Reagan or Vladimir Putin, both of whom have sometimes been called "populist," but it does describe the logic of the parties, movements, and candidates from America's People's Party of 1892 to Marine Le Pen's National Front of 2016. I would, however, take Kazin's characterization one step further and distinguish between leftwing populists like Sanders or

Podemos's Pablo Iglesias and rightwing populists like Trump and the National Front's Le Pen. Leftwing populists champion the people against an elite or an establishment. Theirs is a vertical politics of the bottom and middle arrayed against the top. Rightwing populists champion the people against an elite that they accuse of coddling a third group, which can consist, for instance, of immigrants, Islamists, or African American militants. Leftwing populism is dyadic. Rightwing populism is triadic. It looks upward, but also down upon an out group.

Leftwing populism is historically different from socialist or social democratic movements. It is not a politics of class conflict, and it doesn't necessarily seek the abolition of capitalism. It is also different from a progressive or liberal politics that seeks to reconcile the interests of opposing classes and groups. It assumes a basic antagonism between the people and an elite at the heart of its politics. Rightwing populism, on the other hand, is different from a conservatism that primarily identifies with the business classes against their critics and antagonists below. In its American and Western European versions, it is also different from an authoritarian conservatism that aims to subvert democracy. It operates within a democratic context.

Just as there is no common ideology that defines populism, there is no one constituency that comprises "the people." It can be blue-collar workers, shopkeepers, or students burdened by debt; it can be the poor or the middle class. Equally, there is no common identification of "the establishment." It can vary from the "money power" that the old populists decried to George Wallace's "pointy-headed intellectuals" to the "casta" that Podemos assails. The exact referents of "the people" and "the elite" don't define populism; what defines it is the conflictual relationship between the two—or in the case of rightwing populism the three.

16   The conflict itself turns on a set of demands that the populists make of the elite. These are not ordinary demands that populists believe will be subject to immediate negotiation. The populists believe the demands are worthy and justified, but they don't believe the establishment will be willing to grant them. Sanders wants "Medicare for all" and a $15 minimum wage. If he wanted the Affordable Care Act to cover hearing aids, or to raise the minimum wage to $7.75, that wouldn't define a clash between the people and the establishment. If Trump were to demand an increase in guards along the Mexican border, or if Denmark's People's Party campaigned on a reduction in asylum-seekers, these would not open up a gulf between the people and the elite. But promising a wall that the Mexican government will pay for or the total cessation of immigration—that does establish a frontier.

These kinds of demands define the clash between the people and the establishment. If they are granted in whole or even in part, as when the Democrats in 1896 adopted the People's Party's demand for free silver, or if they abandon them as too ambitious, as Syriza did its demands for renegotiation of Greece's debt, then the populist movement is likely to dissipate or to morph into a normal political party or candidacy. In this sense, American and Western European populist movements have flourished when they are in opposition, but have sometimes suffered identity crises when they have entered government.

The Significance of Populism

The second important feature of the populist campaigns and parties I am describing is that they often function as warning signs of a political crisis. American populist movements have arisen only under very special circumstances. In Europe, populist parties have endured on the fringes at times, because the

European multi-party systems tolerate smaller players. But like American populists, they have won success only under certain circumstances. Those circumstances are times when people see the prevailing political norms—put forward, preserved and defended by the leading segments in the country—as being at odds with their own hopes, fears, and concerns. The populists express these neglected concerns and frame them in a politics that pits the people against an intransigent elite. By doing so, they become catalysts for political change.

On both sides of the Atlantic, the major parties favored increased immigration, only to find that in the United States voters were up in arms about illegal immigration and in Europe about immigrant communities that became seedbeds of crime and later terror. The populist candidates and parties gave voice to these concerns. In Europe, the major parties on the continent embraced the idea of a common currency only to find it fall into disfavor during the Great Recession. In the United States, both parties' leaders embraced "free trade" deals only to discover that much of the public did not support these treaties.

The movements themselves don't often achieve their own objectives. They don't necessarily succeed in providing Medicare for all or protecting workers against global capitalism or the European Union. Their demands may be co-opted by the major parties or they may be thoroughly rejected. But the populists roil the waters. They signal that the prevailing political ideology isn't working and needs repair, and the standard worldview is breaking down. That's why Trump and Sanders are important in America, and why the populist left and right are important in Europe. In what follows, I will describe how the logic of populism has worked and why at this particular moment similar kinds of populist protests are erupting across both sides of the north Atlantic.

The Logic of American Populism
From the People's Party to George Wallace

No one, not even Donald Trump, expected him to get the Republican presidential nomination in 2016. Similarly, no one, including Bernie Sanders, expected that up through the California primary in June, the Vermont senator would still be challenging Hillary Clinton for the Democratic nomination.

Trump's success was initially attributed to his showmanship and celebrity. But as he won primary after primary, political experts saw him playing on racist opposition to Barack Obama's presidency or exploiting a latent sympathy for fascism among downscale white Americans. Sanders's success invited less speculation, but commentators tended to dismiss him as a utopian and to focus on the airy idealism of millennial voters. If that were not sufficient explanation for his success, they emphasized Hillary Clinton's weakness as a frontrunner. It makes more sense, however, to understand Trump and Sanders's success as the latest chapter in the history of American populism.

Populism is an American creation that spread later to Latin America and Europe. While strands of American populism go

back to the Revolution and the Jacksonian War on the Bank of
the United States, it really begins with the People's Party of
the 1890s, which set the precedent for movements that have
popped up periodically. In the United States, in contrast to
Europe, these campaigns have burst forth suddenly and unex-
pectedly. Usually short-lived, nevertheless they have had an
outsized impact. While they seem unusual at the time, they are
very much part of the American political fabric.

Two Kinds of Political Events

While the history of American politics is riven with conflicts—
over slavery, prohibition, the trusts, tariffs, abortion, intervention abroad—it is also dominated for long stretches by an
underlying consensus about government's role in the economy
and abroad. If that consensus doesn't always unite the parties,
it determines the ultimate outcome of political conflict. Thus,
from 1935 to the 1970s, there were occasional debates about
the virtues of a progressive income tax, but American policy
reflected an underlying consensus in favor of it. Progressive tax-
ation was itself part of a broader worldview sometimes described
as New Deal liberalism. It had replaced a worldview that stressed
a far more limited role for government in the economy.

The role of underlying worldviews is characteristic of politics in the United States and Europe, and of all countries that are
governed primarily by consent rather than by force and terror.
In Great Britain, for instance, laissez-faire capitalism, associated with Adam Smith's invisible hand, prevailed for much of
the nineteenth century, but after World War II it was super-
seded by Keynesian economics.

American politics is structured to sustain prevailing worldviews. Its characteristics of winner takes all, first past the post,
single-member districts have encouraged a two-party system.

20   Third-party candidates are often dismissed as "spoilers." Moreover, in deciding on whom to nominate in party primaries, voters and party bigwigs have generally taken electability into account, and in the general election, candidates have generally tried to capture the center and to stay away from being branded as an "extremist." American political history is littered with candidates who proved too extreme for the prevailing consensus of one or the other major parties—think of Fred Harris or Jesse Jackson among Democrats and Tom Tancredo or Pat Robertson among Republicans.

As a result of this two-party tilt toward the center, sharp political differences over underlying socioeconomic issues have tended to get blunted or even ignored, particularly in presidential elections. Campaigns are often fought over fleeting social issues such as temperance or abortion or subsidiary economic issues such as the minimum wage or the deficit. But there are times, when, in the face of dramatic changes in the society and economy or in America's place in the world, voters have suddenly become responsive to politicians or movements that raise issues that major parties have either downplayed or ignored. There are two kinds of such events.

The first are what political scientists call realigning elections. In these, a party or a presidential candidate's challenge to the prevailing worldview causes an upheaval that reorders the existing coalitions and leads to a new majority party. Franklin Roosevelt's campaigns in 1932 and, even more so, 1936 did this, and so did Ronald Reagan's campaign in 1980. Such elections are rare. They are usually precipitated by economic depression or war, and by a succession of political outbursts that challenge, but do not replace, the prevailing worldview. In American politics, these outbursts often take the form of populist candidacies and movements.

These catalytic populists have defined politics in "us vs. them" terms—as struggles of the people against the establishment based on issues and demands that the latter had been sidestepping. The rise of the People's Party was the first major salvo against the worldview of laissez-faire capitalism. Huey Long's Share Our Wealth coincided with Franklin Roosevelt's election in 1932 and helped drive the Roosevelt administration to develop a new politics to sustain its majority. Together, these movements established the populist framework that Bernie Sanders, who described himself both as a democratic socialist and as a progressive, would adopt during his 2016 campaign.

As liberal critics would point out during the 1950s, the People's Party had within it strains of anti-Semitism, racism, and nativism, particularly toward the Chinese, but these were at best secondary elements. Until the movement began to disintegrate, the original People's Party was primarily a movement of the left. The first major instances of rightwing populism would come in the 1930s with Father Charles Coughlin, and then in the 1960s with George Wallace's presidential campaigns. Wallace helped doom the New Deal majority and helped lay the basis for the Reagan realignment of 1980. He created a constituency and a rightwing variety of populism—what sociologist Donald Warren called "middle American radicalism"—that would migrate into the Republican Party and become the basis of Donald Trump's challenge to Republican orthodoxy in 2016.

The People's Party

In May 1891, the legend goes, some members of the Kansas Farmers Alliance, riding back home from a national convention in Cincinnati, came up with the term "populist" to describe the political views that they and other alliance groups in the West and South were developing. The next year, the alliance

22   groups joined hands with the Knights of Labor to form the People's Party that over the next two years challenged the most basic assumptions that guided Republicans and Democrats in Washington. The party would be short-lived, but its example would establish the basis for populism in the United States and Europe.

At the time the populists were meeting in Cincinnati, the leading Republicans and Democrats in the United States were reveling in the progress of American industry and finance. They believed in the self-regulating market as an instrument of prosperity and individual opportunity, and thought government's role should be minimal. Grover Cleveland, who was president from 1884 to 1888 and from 1892 to 1896, railed against government "paternalism." Public sector intervention, he declared in his second inaugural address, "stifles the spirit of true Americanism"; its "functions," he stated, "do not include the support of the people." Government's principal role was to maintain a "sound and stable currency" through upholding the gold standard. Cleveland and his rivals quarreled over the tariff and whether the Democrats were the party of "Rum, Romanism, and Rebellion," but they agreed on the fundamental relationship between government and the economy.

But during these years, farmers in the South and the Plains suffered from a sharp drop in agricultural prices. Farm prices fell two-thirds in the Midwest and South from 1870 to 1890. The Plains, which prospered in the early 1880s, were hit by a ruinous drought in the late 1880s. But unsympathetic railroads, which enjoyed monopoly status, raised the cost of transporting farm produce. Many farmers in the South and the Plains states could barely break even. The small family farm gave way to the large "bonanza" farm, often owned by companies based in the East. Salaries were threatened by low-wage immigrants from China,

Japan, Portugal, and Italy. Farmers who retained their land were burdened by debt. In Kansas, 45 percent of the land had become owned by banks.

The farm revolt began in the 1870s with the Farmer Alliances in the North and South. These were originally fraternal societies, modeled on the Masons, with secret handshakes that bonded the members together. The Southern Alliance began in Texas and spread eastward over the South. In the North, it began in New York, died out, and then was revived in the 1880s in the Plains states. The alliances organized cooperatives to try to control prices, which were increasingly set in distant markets, and they began to pressure legislators to regulate railroad rates. As they became more deeply involved in politics, they began to join forces with the Knights of Labor, the workingman's organization that had been founded in 1869 and that by the early 1880s was the main labor group in the United States. In 1885, the Texas alliance declared in a resolution that it sought a "perfect unity of action" between itself and the Knights of Labor.

While the Grange, a farm advocacy group that started just after the Civil War, foreshadowed later interest groups like the National Farmers Union, the alliances saw themselves representing the "people," including farmers and blue-collar workers, against the "money power" or "plutocracy." That was reflected in their early programs, which included a demand for the incorporation and recognition of labor unions alongside demands for railroad regulation, an end to land speculation, and easy money (through the replacement or supplementing of the gold standard) to ease the burden of debt that the farmers suffered from. Except for a few scattered leaders, the populists were not socialists. They wanted to reform rather than abolish capitalism, and their agent of reform was not the socialist working class, but the loosely conceived idea of "the

24   people." Daniel DeLeon, the head of what was then the coun-
        try's main socialist party, the Socialist Labor Party, criticized
        them as "bourgeois."

        Some of the alliance members backed the Greenback Par-
        ty's presidential slate in 1880 and 1884, but most sought to
        influence the dominant parties in their region. The Southern
        Alliance wanted to transform the Democratic Party, and the
        alliance in the Great Plains wanted to change the Republi-
        cans. In December 1889, the alliances began a series of meet-
        ings to develop a national program. Besides the demands on
        currency and land, the program now also included the nation-
        alization of railroads, a graduated income tax, political reform
        (including the secret ballot and direct election of senators), and
        a "sub-treasury" plan that would allow farmers to borrow money
        from the federal government to store their crops until prices rose
        high enough for them to be profitable.

        When the alliance pressured candidates from the Demo-
        crats and Republicans to endorse this platform, the demands
        proved to be too radical and far-reaching for the major parties.
        In the Plains, Republicans scorned the alliance proposals as
        utopian moralism. "The Decalogue and the golden rule have no
        place in a political campaign," Kansas Republican Senator John
        J. Ingalls wrote. In the South, some Democratic statehouse can-
        didates endorsed the alliance proposals, but once in office they
        rebuffed them. Alliance leaders concluded the Democrats and
        Republicans were in the grip of the plutocracy and that the pop-
        ulists would have to organize their own party. Kansas alliance
        members organized in 1890 a state People's Party that did well
        in that year's elections. Then in 1892, the alliances, along with
        the Knights of Labor and other groups, formed a national Peo-
        ple's Party and nominated James K. Weaver, a former Greenback
        Party presidential candidate, to run for president.

The party held its convention in February in St. Louis, where Minnesota populist Ignatius Donnelly penned a preamble to the platform that won widespread acclaim and became the group's manifesto—what the populists called the nation's "second Declaration of Independence." Donnelly was a former Republican congressman and railroad lobbyist who in the mid-1870s had begun moving leftward and had won acclaim as an author and an orator. In the preamble, Donnelly charged that "the fruits of the toil of millions are boldly stolen to build up the colossal fortunes of a few." Government and the major parties were complicit in this theft. "We charge that the controlling influences dominating both these parties have permitted the existing dreadful conditions to develop without serious effort to prevent or restrain them," Donnelly wrote.

Donnelly's preamble echoed the themes of Jacksonian democracy. "We seek to restore the government of the Republic to the hands of 'the plain people,' with whose class it originated," he wrote. But while the Jackson Democrats wanted to restore popular democracy by *eliminating* the role of government in the economy, Donnelly and the populists—in a challenge to the prevailing laissez-faire worldview—wanted government to actively combat economic injustice. "We believe that the powers of government—in other words, of the people—should be expanded . . . as rapidly and as far as the good sense of an intelligent people and the teachings of experience shall justify, to the end that oppression, injustice, and poverty shall eventually cease in the land."

At the St. Louis convention, Donnelly's platform was enthusiastically endorsed by Georgia's Tom Watson, who had been elected to Congress in 1890 as a Democrat backing the alliance platform. "Never before in the history of the world was there arrayed at the ballot box the contending forces of Democracy and

26 Plutocracy," Watson declared. "Will you stand with the people ... by the side of the other wealth producers of the nation ... or will you stand facing them, and from the plutocratic ranks fire a ballot in support of the old parties and their policies of disorganization, despotism, and death?"

There was always a more conservative strain within the populist movement. In the South, some alliance members cooperated with the parallel Colored Farmers' Alliance, but others did not, and racial issues often divided populists from the Plains and the South. Populists also favored the expulsion of Chinese immigrants, whom businesses had imported to provide cheap labor on western farms and railroads. That was understandable, but their support for exclusion was often colored by racist rhetoric. Kansas populist leader Mary E. Lease warned of a "tide of Mongols." And Watson's *People's Party Paper* denounced the Chinese as "moral and social lepers." But in the 1880s and early 1890s, populist politics was primarily directed upward at the plutocrats. As historian Robert McMath recounts, they were repeatedly accused of being "Molly Maguires, Anarchists, and Communists."

In the 1892 election, the People's Party did remarkably well. Their woefully underfunded presidential candidate received 8 percent of the vote and carried five states. Then in 1893, as Cleveland was taking office, an economic depression took hold, leaving a quarter of Americans unemployed and thousands of farmers bankrupt. Cleveland reaffirmed the gold standard, and to pleas for government aid from farmers, Cleveland's Secretary of Agriculture, Julius Sterling Morton, responded, "The intelligent, practical, and successful farmer needs no aid from the government. The ignorant, impractical, and indolent farmer deserves none."

In the 1894 election, the People's Party's candidates for the House of Representatives won 10 percent of the vote. The party elected 4 congressmen, 4 senators, 21 state executives, and 465 state legislators. With their base in the South and the West, and with Cleveland wildly unpopular, they looked to be on their way to challenging the Democrats as the second party, but the election of 1894 turned out to be the party's swan song.

The populists were done in by the dynamics of the two-party system. In the Plains states, anger against Cleveland turned voters back to the more electable Republicans. In the South, Democrats subdued the People's Party by a combination of cooptation and, in response to the willingness of some populists to court the negro vote, vicious race-baiting. Watson said of the opposition to the People's Party, "The argument against the independent political movement in the South may be boiled down into one word—nigger."

In the wake of 1894, Southern Democrats like South Carolina Senator "Pitchfork" Ben Tillman commonly combined a patina of populist economics and political reform with white supremacy. (Tillman's nickname came from his promise in 1984 that if he were elected, he would go to Washington and "stick a pitchfork in Grover Cleveland's old fat ribs.") Watson himself and Texas's James "Cyclone" Davis, while continuing to support populist economics, became allies of the Ku Klux Klan.

But the biggest damage occurred on the national stage. In 1896, the Democrats nominated Nebraskan William Jennings Bryan and adopted key planks of the populist platform, including monetization of silver ("free silver"!), the regulation of the railroads and other corporations, and a restriction on "foreign pauper labor." At its convention, the People's Party chose to endorse Bryan rather than to run a candidate of its own. In the 1896 election, the populist vote migrated to the major parties. To make matters worse, the populists also lost their blue-collar ally when the Knights of Labor fell apart and was

28   replaced by the interest-group oriented American Federation of Labor. The People's Party limped along and finally collapsed after the 1908 election when Watson, running as its presidential candidate, received 0.19 percent of the vote.

But during their heyday from 1885 to 1894, the populists of the alliances and the People's Party had a profound effect on American and, as it turned out, Latin American and European politics. They developed the logic of populism—the concept of a "people" arrayed against an elite that refused to grant necessary reforms. In American politics, they were an early sign of the inadequacy of the two parties' view of government and the economy.

The populists were the first to call for government to regulate and even nationalize industries that were integral to the economy, like the railroads; they wanted government to reduce the economic inequality that capitalism, when left to its own devices, was creating; and they wanted to reduce the power of business in determining the outcome of elections. Populism had an immediate impact on the politics of some progressive Democrats like Bryan, and even on Republicans like Theodore Roosevelt and Robert La Follette. Eventually, much of the populists' agenda—from the graduated income tax to a version of the sub-treasury plan—was incorporated into the New Deal and into the outlook of New Deal liberalism.

Huey Long's Share Our Wealth

In the 1920s, while much of Europe suffered from economic and political instability, partly as a result of post-World War I reparations and gold-based finance, the American economy enjoyed a boom. Republican business boosterism and rugged individualism dominated politics. But the stock market crash of 1929 and the Great Depression that followed shattered the public's confidence in the free market, as well as in Republican rule, and helped to bring about a new Democratic majority.

Franklin Roosevelt and the Democrats won a landslide victory in 1932, but not by repudiating the Republicans' overall outlook on government and the economy. In the campaign, Roosevelt criticized Republican incumbent Herbert Hoover for overspending and promised to cut the government bureaucracy by 25 percent and balance the budget. Once in office, Roosevelt actually tried to make good on this promise through the Government Economy Act, which cut more than $500 million from the budget mainly out of veterans' benefits and government salaries.

Roosevelt did move aggressively during his first two years to reform banking and provide jobs through new government programs. He created a National Recovery Administration that was supposed to work out corporatist arrangements between business and labor and stem cutthroat price competition. But Roosevelt did not directly address economic inequality, which had grown during the years of the Republican majority and which progressive economists believed lay at the heart of the crash and the Depression. It took pressure from outside to get Roosevelt to do this, and much of it came from Louisiana politician Huey Long. Long created a populist movement that Democrats feared would threaten Roosevelt's reelection and possibly even the existence of the Democratic Party.

Long grew up in Winn, Louisiana, a small, poor farming town that was a hotbed of populist and socialist support. He carried on the populist tradition, campaigning for governor on the slogan, "Every man a king, but no man wears a crown," and railing against oil companies and the "money power." Elected governor in 1928, he funded Louisiana's roads, healthcare

30 system, and schools, while exempting low-income people from taxes and proposing (and eventually getting) an extraction tax on oil companies. He didn't repudiate racism, but he didn't actively encourage it either. "Don't say I am working for niggers, I'm not. I'm for the poor man—all poor men," he declared. Dictatorial and charismatic, he was an exemplar of the populist who became the unifying force holding "the people" together. One reporter wrote of Long's constituents, "They worship the ground he walks on."

Long got elected to the senate in 1930, and in 1932 he backed Roosevelt for president. But soon after Roosevelt took office, Long broke with him. He spoke out and voted against the Government Economy Act. He claimed it was the work of "Mr. Morgan" and "Mr. Rockefeller." In February 1934, Long announced on radio the formation of a Share Our Wealth Society. Its centerpiece was a proposal to cap a family's wealth at $5 million and income at $1 million through taxes, and to use the revenue to provide every family a "household estate" that would be enough for "a home, an automobile, a radio, and ordinary conveniences" and a guaranteed annual income to "maintain a family in comfort," as well as an old-age pension.

Long's tax rates on the wealthy were draconian, but they still would not have produced the revenue necessary for what he promised. Roosevelt's allies in the media mocked Long's proposal. *The New Republic* sent Long a mock questionnaire about the details of his plan, asking, "Upon what statistics of economic studies do you base your conclusions?" But the very extravagance of Long's plan established a political divide between him and the powers-that-be that could not easily be bridged. It defined the movement's radicalism the way free silver, the sub-treasury plan, and the nationalization of railroads defined the People's Party.

Long's Share Our Wealth clubs—more than 27,000 had started by the following February—functioned not only as local political organizations but as the basis for a new political party. They were often run out of churches and schools. In addition, Long boasted of a mailing list of more than 7.5 million. Long's most active base, like that of the People's Party and subsequent populist movements, was not among the very poor. It was among the middle class, who feared that they would be cast down by the Depression into the ranks of the very poor. Historian Alan Brinkley wrote of Long's followers:

> Having gained a foothold in the world of bourgeois respectability, they stood in danger of being plunged back into what they viewed as an abyss of powerlessness and dependence. It was that fear that made the middle class, even more than those who were truly rootless and indigent, a politically volatile group.

Roosevelt and the Democrats feared Long's candidacy. In 1935, the Democratic National Party did a secret poll in which they determined that if Long ran on a Third-party ticket against Roosevelt in 1936, he could win between three and four million votes and throw the election to the Republicans. That fear was an important factor in Roosevelt and the Democrats joining forces that year to pass what was called "the Second New Deal." Unlike the first, it dealt directly with the issue of economic inequality that Long had repeatedly raised.

On June 19, the Senate passed the Social Security Act, which provided old-age pensions and unemployment compensation. On the same day, Roosevelt surprised Congress by proposing a tax reform measure to encourage "a wider distribution of wealth." He imposed levies on large businesses and raised taxes on the wealthy and on large inheritances. Long criticized

32   the proposals as being weak, but they were widely portrayed as "soaking the rich." Roosevelt also incorporated populist rhetoric in his presidential campaign that year, championing the "average man" against the "economic royalists."

As it turned out, Roosevelt did not have to fear Long's candidacy. In September 1935, the Kingfish was assassinated in Baton Rouge. And in 1936, Roosevelt won another landslide. But Long had a significant influence over the New Deal and over American politics. He and his movement pushed Congress to adopt programs that became pillars of American policy for the next four decades. Long brought the New Deal's outlook into line with the public's underlying concern about the inequality of wealth and power.

George Wallace

The '60s were thought of as an era of ferment on the left. In Europe, there were the May–June 1968 protests in France and the Hot Autumn in Italy in 1969. In the United States, it was the time of civil rights, black power, anti-war, feminism, and environmentalism. But it was also when a rightwing populist, George Wallace, acting in opposition to civil rights rulings and legislation, blew a large hole in the roof that New Deal liberalism had erected over American politics.

The New Deal had rested on a tacit alliance between liberal Democrats and conservative Southern Democrats who resisted any legislation that might challenge white supremacy. As a result, key New Deal legislation, including the Social Security and Minimum Wage acts, were formulated to exclude Southern blacks from their benefits. But after World War II, northern Democrats, propelled by the Cold War's ideological struggle, *Brown v. Board of Education*, and a powerful civil rights movement, embraced the black American cause.

As the party of Abraham Lincoln, Republicans had traditionally been receptive to black civil rights, and the Republican leadership in Congress supported Lyndon Johnson's Civil Rights and Voting Rights acts of 1964 and 1965. Barry Goldwater was an early dissenter, but in the 1964 presidential election, Johnson easily defeated him. Johnson's victory did not, however, signal widespread support for his civil rights initiatives, and after he passed the Voting Rights Act and launched the War on Poverty, a popular backlash grew. Wallace turned the backlash into a populist crusade.

Wallace was raised in a rural small town in Alabama. His father and grandfather dabbled in politics. They were New Deal Democrats under Roosevelt's spell. Wallace would eventually make his name as an arch-segregationist, but he was initially a populist Democrat like Long for whom race was strictly a secondary consideration. When he was a delegate to the 1948 Democratic Convention, he didn't join the Dixiecrat walkout in protest of the party's civil rights platform. He initially ran for governor in 1958 as a New Deal Democrat and lost against a candidate backed by the Ku Klux Klan. After that, he pledged, "I will never be outniggered again."

In 1962, Wallace ran again and this time he won as a proponent of "segregation now, segregation tomorrow, segregation forever." In 1963, he gained notoriety when he attempted to block two black students from registering at the University of Alabama. In 1964, he ran in the Democratic primaries against Johnson's surrogates in Wisconsin, Indiana, and Maryland and got about a third of the vote—as high as 43 percent in Maryland, where he carried 15 of 23 counties. In 1968, he ran as an independent against Nixon and Humphrey. In early October, he was ahead of Humphrey in the polls, but in the end, he got 13.5 percent of the vote and carried five states in the South. In 1972, he

34 ran as a Democrat, and stood a chance of taking the nomination when an assassin shot and crippled him while he was campaigning in May for the Maryland primary.

Wallace emphasized his opposition to racial integration, but he framed it as a defense of the average (white) American against the tyranny of Washington bureaucrats. Big government was imposing its way on the average person. Appearing on *Meet the Press* in 1967, Wallace summed up his candidacy:

> There's a backlash against big government in this country. This is a movement of the people. . . . And I think that if the politicians get in the way a lot of them are going to get run over by this average man in the street—this man in the textile mill, this man in the steel mill, this barber, this beautician, the policeman on the beat . . . the little businessman.

Wallace opposed busing—which became a major issue after a 1971 Supreme Court order upheld it as a means to achieve desegregation—because it was breaking up working-class neighborhoods, and he attacked the white liberals who promoted it as hypocrites who refused to subject their children to what they insisted that working- and middle-class kids be subjected to. "They are building a bridge over the Potomac for all the white liberals fleeing to Virginia," he declared.

Wallace was not, however, a political conservative. On domestic issues that didn't directly touch on race, Wallace ran as a New Deal Democrat. In his campaign brochure in 1968, he boasted that in Alabama, he had increased spending on education, welfare, roads, and agriculture. When he was asked in 1967 who he would appoint to his cabinet if he were elected, he said he would consider either AFL-CIO head George Meany or Leonard Woodcock, the head of the United Auto Workers. He also drew a line between the people and the very rich and powerful. Campaigning in Florida, he said, "We're sick and tired of the average citizen being taxed to death while these multibillionaires like the Rockefellers and the Fords and the Mellons and Carnegies go without paying taxes." Wallace, like Long, was often called fascist, but he was a rightwing populist in the tradition of the post-1896 Tom Watson. When protesters accused him of being a fascist, Wallace, who served in World War II, responded, "I was killing fascists when you punks were in diapers."

Like Wallace, his supporters were a mix of left and right in their convictions. In 1976, sociologist Donald Warren published a study of what he called "middle American radicals," or MARs. On the basis of extensive surveys conducted in 1971–72 and 1975, Warren defined a distinct political group that was neither left nor right, liberal nor conservative. MARs "feel the middle class has been seriously neglected," Warren wrote. They see "government as favoring both the rich and poor simultaneously."

Warren's MARs held conservative positions on poverty and racial issues. They rejected racial busing and welfare agencies as examples of "the rich [giving] in to the demands of the poor, and the middle income people have to pay the bill." They disliked the national government, but they also thought corporations "have too much power" and were "too big." They favored many liberal programs. They wanted government to guarantee jobs to everyone. They supported price (but not wage) control, Medicare, some kind of national health insurance, federal aid to education, and Social Security.

Warren found that MARs represented about a quarter of the electorate. They were on average more male than female; they had a high school but not a college education; their income fell in the middle, or slightly below; they had skilled or semi-skilled blue-collar jobs, or clerical or sales white-collar work. When

36 Warren grouped by income and education the other groups he surveyed into "lower income," "average middles," "high education middles," and "affluents," he found that of all of them the MARs were most likely to contemplate voting for George Wallace in 1972. A Gallup study of the demographics of the 1968 Wallace vote found his constituency to be identical to that of Warren's MARs.

In other words, Wallace's base was among voters who saw themselves as "middle class"—the American equivalent of "the people"—and who saw themselves locked in conflict with those below and above. Like Wallace, they remained New Deal liberals in many of their views, but not on matters that bore on race or law and order. In these cases, they adamantly rejected the welfare and busing and affirmative action policies that 1972 Democratic presidential candidate George McGovern and many liberal Democrats favored. They had begun the political journey from Democrat to Independent to Republican that would finally conclude in the 1994 congressional elections.

Wallace, like Long, was a movement unto himself. When he was shot and forced to drop out of the presidential campaign, it ended his attempt to transform American politics. He would run again in 1976 but would be eclipsed by another Southern politician, Jimmy Carter. Attempts by conservatives to retain his American Independent Party flopped. He would serve as governor again, and would repudiate and apologize for his own opposition to racial integration. He would end his career much as he began—as a New Deal Democrat. But Wallace and his followers had already had a profound influence on the two-party system.

Wallace's campaigns were the opening wedge in the realignment of the parties in the South. The Republicans would subsequently accommodate Wallace's positions on big government, welfare, busing, and affirmative action. And Nixon had already begun to do that. As Kevin Phillips understood in his prescient 1969 book, *The Emerging Republican Majority*, Wallace's votes would migrate to the Republican Party. In 1972, Nixon's percentage vote against McGovern closely resembled the total of Nixon and Wallace's votes in 1968 in 45 of 50 states. In 14 states, the percentages were almost identical.

The Democratic and Republican coalitions that would emerge after Wallace's 1968 run and McGovern's 1972 campaign would be significantly different from the coalitions of the New Deal era. From 1932 through 1960, the two parties' support could roughly be arrayed in a pyramid with income and education moving upward. Democrats, as the party of the "common man," took up most of the bottom two-thirds. That allowed the Democrats to win most of the elections.

In 1972, many white voters in the lower and middle segments of the pyramid would begin shifting to the Republicans, while many professionals—from nurses and teachers to engineers and architects—who had been loyal Republicans, but who had been touched by the new left movements of the '60s, and had expected but not found autonomy and satisfaction in their work, would begin voting for the Democrats. They became critics of unregulated capitalism, and their descendants would provide much of Bernie Sanders's support. The Democrats began building an odd coalition of the minority poor with upper-middle-class whites. There would no longer be a clear demarcation between the parties on income and education.

The transformation of the coalitions would be delayed by the Watergate scandal and wouldn't fully come to fruition until 1980 or even 1994, when the Republicans would win both houses of Congress. Wallace's populist candidacies, far more than Goldwater's, set this process in motion. His campaigns would lead

38   to Republicans adopting Wallace's stand on government and state's rights, along with an opportunistic imitation of his own populist anti-elitist politics (directed at "Washington"). But then Pat Buchanan in his 1992 and 1996 campaigns and Trump in his 2016 campaign would draw on the unruly populism of Wallace's middle American radicals and would mobilize it against the Republicans' more traditional supporters.

Neoliberalism and Its Enemies: Perot, Buchanan, the Tea Party, and Occupy Wall Street

New Deal liberalism reigned from 1932 to 1968. The New Deal did not represent, as some critics claimed, a repudiation of capitalism, but an attempt to save and reform it, after the laissez-faire, pro-business policies of Republican administrations had helped to bring about the financial crash and the Great Depression. The New Deal approach, which used government to counter capitalism's tendencies toward unemployment, inequality, monopoly, and environmental pollution, helped produce several decades of post-World War II prosperity.

George Wallace's populist crusade undermined the Democrats' political majority, which depended upon the support of Southern states, but it didn't discredit the New Deal liberal worldview of government and the economy. Wallace, after all, was a New Deal liberal himself. That discrediting would happen during the 1970s, as the United States faced economic conditions that appeared to justify a new conception of the relationship between government and the economy. The business community would champion this new conception, and Republicans, many of whom had reluctantly backed the New

40   Deal—Goldwater famously called the Eisenhower administration's budget a "dime store New Deal"—would embrace the new approach.

Democrats would initially object to the new conception, but by the 1990s would in some cases come around to its essentials, or in others be forced to do so by a powerful Republican opposition. The approach was initially called "supply-side economics," and that term fits part of it. Leftwing political scientists have also called it "neoliberalism" and have drawn a connection to similar politics in Europe. The term is ambiguous, because while liberalism in the United States refers often to New Deal liberalism, it refers in Europe to classical free-market economics. But I am going to use it because the result in both cases is equivalent.

In the United States, neoliberalism meant the modification, but not wholesale abandonment, of New Deal liberalism— support for the New Deal safety net, but beyond that, priority to market imperatives—while in Europe, it meant the partial return to an older free market liberalism. The United States is still in an era dominated by this neoliberal worldview, but it has come under attack from populist politicians and movements— from Ross Perot and Pat Buchanan in the early 1990s to the Tea Party and Occupy Wall Street in the 2010s.

The Triumph of Neoliberalism

The origins of neoliberalism go back to the global challenges that American business began to face in the early 1970s, as Western Europe and Japan had rebuilt their factories and were able to compete effectively with American manufacturers. That became evident when for the first time in the twentieth century, the United States ran a trade deficit in 1971. With developing nations beginning to build steel mills as well as textile plants,

American producers were also faced with global overcapacity in
key industries like steel, shoes, textiles, shipbuilding, chemi-
cals, televisions, automobiles, and refrigerators. (The list has
continued to grow over the years.) The combination of growing
competition and global overcapacity was an important factor in
driving down profit rates for American producers. According
to economic historian Robert Brenner, from 1965 to 1973, rates
of profit fell 40.9 percent in manufacturing and 23.1 percent in
non-manufacturing.

During the decades of postwar prosperity, business had
acquiesced in steady wage increases, especially in unionized industries, because they could be defrayed through rising
prices, productivity, and sales. But by the early 1970s, businesses were also increasingly worried about wage pressure
from below that was threatening their rates of profit. A major
labor wave had occurred from 1965 to 1973, almost doubling the
number of strikes that had occurred in the previous decade. In
addition, businesses increasingly feared an alliance between the
unions and New Left militants. In a special issue on the Seven-
ties, *Business Week* voiced fears of a challenge to "corporations
and the middle- and upper-bracket income earners" from "the
blacks, the labor unions, and the young."

American businesses responded to these threats by
adopting a hard line against unionization, sometimes even in
violation of labor law. They moved plants to right-to-work
states and overseas. They created an extensive lobbying net-
work in Washington—pro-business think tanks and policy
groups as well as the newly established Business Roundtable of
corporate CEOs—to promote tax cuts and the repeal or weak-
ening of regulations. They lobbied for trade deals that not only
removed tariff barriers to American exports, but eased overseas
investment by protecting American firms from expropriation.

42   Business wasn't the main force behind the 1965 Immigration and Nationality Act, but it certainly took advantage of it. Through family reunification, the act led to a flood of new immigrants, including unskilled labor from Latin America and Asia. Agribusiness, food processing, meatpacking, construction, hotel, restaurant, and other service businesses used these workers, many of whom were undocumented or not eligible for citizenship, to push down wages and to resist or undermine unions. Businesses would later fight any attempts to penalize them for hiring undocumented workers.

One example is what happened with Midwestern meatpacking plants. According to a *New York Times* report in 2001, "Until 15 or 20 years ago, meatpacking plants in the United States were staffed by highly paid, unionized employees who earned about $18 an hour, adjusted for inflation. Today, the processing and packing plants are largely staffed by low-paid non-union workers from places like Mexico and Guatemala. Many of them start at $6 an hour." According to a Pew report, by 2005 between 20 and 25 percent of the workers in these plants were undocumented.

There wasn't widespread public support for these measures. The 1965 immigration bill was not popular, and by the late 1990s, states had begun passing referenda against illegal immigration that were also directed implicitly at legal immigrants. There was also public skepticism about trade deals, and opposition to American firms moving plants overseas, as I remember once attending a convention of the Christian Coalition, a major organization of conservative evangelicals run by two pro-business Republicans, Pat Robertson and Ralph Reed. Robertson and Reed got the organization to endorse the North American Free Trade Agreement (NAFTA), but when I talked to the group's rank-and-file I found almost universal opposition to it. A November 1993 Gallup poll found opposition to NAFTA at 46 percent against with only 38 percent for. In January 1999, a Pew poll found 54 percent of the public opposed to granting China most-favored-nation trading status and 32 percent for.

In spite of public skepticism, business carried the day in the Republican Party—and eventually in the Democratic Party as well. Operatives crafted a majority coalition that was composed of the traditional Republican business class, small businesses and farmers, and white working-class voters who had began fleeing the Democratic Party because of its support for civil rights, feminism, and the secular counterculture. There was an implicit arrangement by which the major business lobbies would acquiesce in Republican opposition to abortion, gun control, or affirmative action in exchange for working-class support for reductions in regulations and taxes.

The one area in which Republican business and the new white working-class Republicans could wholeheartedly agree was cutting social spending. Businesses generally favored any spending cuts that would lower pressure to raise taxes on them and their stockholders. The working and middle classes, with some justification, believed they would have to pay the bulk of the taxes to support programs that they believed would primarily benefit minorities and the poor and not themselves. This opposition to spending (and to any tax increases thought to support it) was capsulized in a general opposition to "Washington" and to "big government."

Many Democrats initially resisted the neoliberal agenda, but attempts in the first two years of the Carter administration to strengthen labor law, progressive tax reform, consumer regulation, and campaign finance reform were beaten back by Republicans and the business lobbies. In addition, Democratic

44   policy makers found themselves hamstrung by the combination of growing unemployment and inflation—the result in the latter case of rising energy and food prices. This "stagflation" (stagnation + inflation) defied the usual Keynesian demand-side remedies, and there was little support for going beyond those remedies to extensive price controls. By the late 1970s, the Carter administration had acquiesced to supply-side business tax cuts and to a monetarist strategy of using high interest rates and rising unemployment to curb inflation.

Over the next 12 years, Democrats, led by the "new Democrats," would accept other key aspects of the neoliberal agenda, including trade pacts like NAFTA that eased foreign investment, deregulation of finance, and immigration measures to accommodate unskilled and later highly skilled guest workers. Democrats would continue to fight Republicans on some social spending measures and on income and inheritance tax changes, but once the Republicans won control of Congress in 1994, Democrats would be forced into uncomfortable compromises. Attempts to revive labor legislation would simply fail. Election battles would almost invariably leave the heights of the neoliberal approach untouched, and focus instead on social policies such as abortion or gun control and on relatively marginal differences over social spending and taxes.

The key contention that sustained the neoliberal agenda was that the older New Deal liberalism, by focusing on raising consumer demand and reducing inequality, would stifle growth and reduce Americans' standard of living. By contrast, the neoliberal and supply-side agenda, while not directly confronting economic inequality, promised to spur economic growth, which would benefit all Americans. As Ronald Reagan, borrowing from John Kennedy, put it in the 1980 campaign, "a rising tide will lift all boats." Similar kinds of arguments would be made in Europe

by the "Third Way" centrists, who were partially inspired by
Tory Prime Minister Margaret Thatcher.

But even by the late 1980s, reality on the ground appeared to contradict these claims of widespread prosperity. In the 1980s, growth and employment lagged behind that of previous decades. The shape of the economy also began to change under Reagan. The Reagan and Bush administrations ignored calls for an industrial policy that would protect and help expand America's manufacturing sector. Instead, Reagan's reliance on high interest rates and an overvalued dollar helped accelerate the decline of America's manufacturing industries, fueling the growth of finance and financial services.

By the end of the '80s, large swaths of domestically based industries, including consumer electronics, machine tools, and textiles, had disappeared. The jobs in these industries were replaced by lower-wage service sector and higher-wage professional-level jobs—many either employing or employed by information technology—which created an indentation in the middle of the workforce and a rise in inequality. Economic historian Peter Temin argues that these neoliberal policies created a "dual economy" composed of a high-wage FTE (finance, technology and electronics) sector and a low-wage one of semi-skilled and unskilled workers that straddled a shrinking middle-income group of manufacturing and white-collar jobs.

Along the same lines, economist Stephen Rose has shown that the rising difference in income and wealth prevailed not just between the 1 percent and the 99 percent, but between the top 30 percent—including a growing upper middle class—and the bottom 70 percent. These trends, reinforced by further financial deregulation, an overvalued dollar, and regressive tax policies, would continue up through the onset of the Great Recession and fuel discontent among the middle and lower-middle classes,

46   many of whom felt cast aside by the move toward a post-industrial economy heavily dependent on finance and financial services. (As I will recount, something very similar happened in Western Europe.)

The first visible crisis came in 1991, when the U.S. suffered from a peculiar recession that seemed to drag on for four more years in joblessness and wage stagnation. In addition, many Americans were troubled by the continuing loss of manufacturing jobs to Japan and Western Europe, and the rapid rise in illegal immigration in the Southwest. Public opinion expert Daniel Yankelovich wrote, "Even though they can't put their finger on it, [people] fear something is fundamentally wrong with the U.S. economy."

When party leaders' promises—that free trade deals would create far more jobs than they would threaten, that immigration measures would stop the flood of immigrants entering the country illegally, and that financial deregulation would have no ill effects—proved false, it sparked a populist challenge to the prevailing consensus. That challenge came in the 1992 and 1996 elections from Texas businessman Ross Perot, and from former Nixon and Reagan aide Pat Buchanan. Perot represented a left and center-left populism, and Buchanan a challenge from the right, but like other American populists, they didn't fit the conventional conflict between Democrats and Republicans or between liberals and conservatives. Instead, they arose precisely because the leading Democrats and Republicans were ignoring popular concerns about American manufacturing, immigration, and lobbying in Washington.

Ross Perot

Perot grew up in Texarkana, a small farming town in East Texas that used to be a stopover for People's Party agitators. His father was a cotton broker who struggled to make a living during the Great Depression. Following two years at junior college, Perot talked a retiring senator from neighboring Arkansas into appointing him to the Naval Academy. After graduating, Perot spent two years at sea before obtaining an early discharge in order to go into business.

Perot began his career selling and servicing mainframe computers for IBM, but in 1962, he set up his own data processing company, Electronic Data Systems, which he turned into a multi-billion dollar enterprise. In 1985, he sold it to General Motors with the idea that he and EDS would have a leadership role within the faltering company, but when GM's management ignored him, he left and started Perot Systems. The experience helped turn him into an outspoken critic of corporate America and of the Republican and Democratic politicians who had coddled it.

Perot had been an active Republican. In 1968, he loaned members of EDS to the Nixon campaign. But he was a moderate. In Texas, he devoted himself to improving the state's school systems, and particularly those schools that primarily catered to minorities. He was pro-choice and in favor of gay rights and gun control. He was not viscerally opposed to government intervention in the economy like some hardline conservatives, and after his experience with GM, Perot became convinced that government had to take a stronger and more effective hand in steering the economy. That put him directly at odds with the Bush administration, which condemned "industrial policy." In the spring of 1992, Perot gave his consent to his followers putting his name on the ballot for an independent run for the presidency.

Perot portrayed himself as an unpaid servant of the people against a corrupt government and inept corporate hierarchy. America's CEOs like GM's Roger Smith, he argued, were too

48   concerned with quarterly returns, and political leaders with poll findings. The White House and Congress, he charged, were under the grip of an army of lobbyists, including those representing foreign companies and governments, which had descended on Washington over the prior two decades. Perot promised to reverse the relationship between the people and their government. "We own this country," Perot told the National Press Club in March 1992:

> Government should come from us. It now comes at us with a propaganda machine in Washington that Hitler's propaganda chief, Goebbels, would have just envied. We've got to put the country back in the control of the owners. And in plain Texas talk, it's time to take out the trash and clean out the barn, or it's going to be too late.

Like a conventional pre-Reaganite Republican, Perot wanted to balance the budget. But he also wanted to prevent corporations from transferring their jobs overseas, and opposed NAFTA. "The White House is all excited about the new trade agreement with Mexico. This agreement will move the highest paid blue-collared jobs in the U.S. to Mexico. This is going to create serious damage to our tax base during this critical period. We have got to manufacture here and not there to keep our tax base intact," Perot told the Press Club. Perot promised that he would restore American manufacturing jobs and that consumers would once again see American products in stores. "We need jobs here, and we must manufacture here if we wish to remain a superpower. We must stop shipping manufacturing jobs overseas and once again make the words 'Made in the USA' the world's standard of excellence," he declared.

Perot had been skeptical of the Bush administration's decision to intervene militarily to oust Iraq from Kuwait. He thought

the United States had to stress burden sharing with its allies in
Europe and Asia and to focus on rebuilding its economy. "Our
highest foreign policy priority is to get our house in order and
make America work again," he declared. To do that, he favored
public investments that would target "industries of the future"
after the manner of Japan's ministry of international trade and
industry. He dismissed the objections of free market advocates.
"Don't they realize that the biogenetics industry is the result
of our federally funded research universities and the National
Institutes of Health?" he declared.

To reclaim Washington for the people, Perot advocated
tightening the restrictions on former officials becoming lobbyists, reforming campaign spending to limit contributions,
shortening the campaign season, making voting more acces-
sible ("Why do we have elections on Tuesday? Working fellows
can't get there"), and using computers to create "electronic town
halls" where the nation could learn about and debate issues.
Perot promised to overcome the "gridlock" (a term he popular-
ized) between Republicans and Democrats. He pledged that he
would be the "servant" and that the people would be the "boss."
But in Perot's contempt for Congress and the political parties
and his proposal for electronic plebiscites, he was in effect putting himself in a position of a super-president who would have
an unmediated relationship to the American people. Like Long,
he was seen as "dictatorial," even by his own voters.

Perot quickly climbed to the top of the polls. In a CNN/
Time poll in May he had 33 percent to 28 percent for Bush and 24
percent for Clinton. But Perot was not prepared for the kind of
intensive questioning that the press then subjected him to. Perot's own conspiratorial streak also undid him. He had trouble
confirming a claim that the Black Panther Party, on contract
with the Viet Cong, had once tried to break into his house. As he

50   began to falter in the polls in July, and after his campaign man-
     ager resigned, Perot suddenly quit the race. But on October 1,
     Perot reentered the race. His eccentricities had already doomed
     his chance to win, but his exceptional performance in the
     debates—he memorably warned in the October 15 debate that
     NAFTA would create a "great sucking sound" on American
     jobs—kept him in the race until the end. He won 19 percent of
     the vote overall and more than 25 percent in nine states. In an
     exit poll, 40 percent of voters said that they would have voted
     for him if they thought he had had a chance to win.

     Perot took voters almost equally from the Democrats and
     the Republicans. In focus groups he did for Perot, Frank Luntz
     found that "not once did a Perot supporter identify either
     Perot or himself as liberal or conservative." In November exit
     polls, Perot did best among voters who identified themselves
     as "moderates" and "independents." Pollster Stanley Greenberg
     characterized his voters as representing "the radical middle—
     split evenly between conservatives and liberal/moderates." His
     highest numbers were among voters who believed their finan-
     cial situation was "worse now than in 1988." Perot was more in
     the tradition of the original populists and of Long, but his voters
     had something of the Wallace rightwing populist outlook. In a
     post-election survey, Greenberg found that a majority of Perot's
     voters thought that "business corporations" did not "strike a
     fair balance between making profits and serving the public," but
     they also strongly supported the idea that "It's the middle class,
     not the poor, who really get a raw deal today." (It was not sur-
     prising that Perot voters by two-to-one subsequently backed
     Republicans in the 1994 congressional races, which the GOP
     swept.)

     In his initial campaign speeches, Perot started off with an
     attack on the deficit, but later in the campaign, he began by

attacking trade deals and runaway shops and K Street lobbyists. That resonated with his voters. According to the exit polls
in November, when voters were asked, "Overall, would you say
U.S. trade with other countries creates more jobs for the U.S.,
loses more jobs for the U.S., or has no effect on U.S. jobs?" Perot
voters said by 49 to 35 percent that trade loses more jobs. As
Ruy Teixeira and Guy Molyneux noted in their 1993 election
study, "Some of Perot's biggest applause lines in the televised
debates—both as measured in the studio and among viewers in
the home—were those that bluntly asserted the need to limit
the influence of foreign lobbyists and take a tougher U.S. trade
stance." He and his vote represented the first clear repudiation
of the neoliberal agenda.

Pat Buchanan

The same year that Perot ran, former Nixon and Reagan speech-
writer Pat Buchanan challenged George H. W. Bush for the
Republican nomination. He ran against Bush primarily from the
right, criticizing the president for reneging on his vow not to
raise taxes. But Buchanan also criticized Bush for overextending
America's commitments abroad and for neglecting America's
economic challenge from Japan and Western Europe. "We can't
just let foreign imports come in here and rob us of American
jobs," Buchanan declared in a campaign speech." Buchanan got a
surprising 38 percent in New Hampshire, a sure sign of Republican dissatisfaction with Bush, but because he was seen as a
protest candidate, Buchanan failed to top that in any of the subsequent primaries.

Buchanan decided to run again in 1996. This time, he took
aim more explicitly at the neoliberal agenda that Republicans and
Democrats shared. On the eve of the campaign Buchanan wrote,
"As transnational corporations compete ever more ferociously,

52 First World workers become expendable. . . . What has global competition done for the quality of life of Middle America? What, after all, is an economy for, if not for its people?" In another column, he warned, "The battle for the future will be as much a battle within the parties as it will be between the parties, a battle between the hired men of the Money Power who long abandoned the quaint but useless old ideas of nationhood—and populists, patriots and nationalists who want no part of [Secretary of the Treasury under Bill Clinton] Robert Rubin's world." During his campaign, he fired salvos at corporate America and Wall Street. "There will be no more GATT deals done for the benefit of Wall Street bankers," Buchanan promised during a campaign stop in Youngstown. And of NAFTA: "You don't force Americans making ten bucks an hour to compete with Mexican workers who have to work for a dollar an hour." At the same time as immigration was becoming a big issue in Europe, Buchanan was also the first major presidential candidate to single out illegal immigration. He promised, in fact, to stop immigration altogether. "A country that loses control of its borders isn't really a country anymore," he declared.

Buchanan, who famously described his campaign as rallying "peasants with pitchforks" against the "establishment," astonished pundits in Washington as well as party leaders by winning the Alaska and Louisiana caucuses, coming within two points of favored Senator Bob Dole in Iowa, and then winning the New Hampshire primary. But after New Hampshire, party leaders and pundits closed ranks behind Dole, and Buchanan failed to win another primary. His failure was partly due to voters' seeing him as they did in 1992 as a protest candidate. He had never, after all, held an elective office. He was pugnacious, eloquent, funny, and at times nasty and at other times generous, but he was not presidential.

The collapse of Buchanan's candidacy was also due to
what happened to the American economy. Like Perot in 1992,
Buchanan initially benefited from a flagging economy. Even by
early 1996, the United States had not fully recovered from what
had been called a "jobless recovery" and lagging wage growth.
By the spring of 1996, however, unemployment was dropping
below 5 percent, and real income had begun to rise. Clinton
would cite the awakened economy that year to defeat Dole in the
November election, but even by the late spring, it had undercut
Buchanan's candidacy.

With the economy booming in the late 1990s, neoliberalism seemed to be working. The gap between the very rich and
everyone else was growing, legal and illegal immigration was
soaring, and America's trade deficit was increasing, but neither
Perot, who ran again in 1996 as the Reform Party candidate, nor
Buchanan, who ran again in 2000 as the Reform Party candidate, could get any traction. And what doubts the early dot-com
recession of 2001 would have sown about neoliberalism were
overshadowed by the September 11 terrorist attack and the
Iraq War. But Perot and Buchanan had nonetheless demon-
strated the potential for a revolt against neoliberalism among
the "middle American radicals." The complaints that Perot and
Buchanan voiced would be heard again after the financial crash
of 2008.

The Tea Party

Like the crash of 1929 that led to the Great Depression, the
global financial crisis of 2008 was rooted in long-term, systemic problems. Asian countries were sending back dollars acquired from trade surpluses. With the high-tech boom
exhausted, and manufacturing still generally plagued by global
overcapacity, these dollars were directly or indirectly fueling

54   consumer debt, particularly in housing. The housing boom
       was sustaining demand in an economy that might have other-
       wise slowed. When the housing bubble burst in 2007, millions
       lost their homes and financial institutions were put at risk. A
       steep recession followed. But the crash was also precipitated by
       the politics of neoliberalism—by financial deregulation under
       Carter, Reagan, and Clinton, and lax regulation under George
       W. Bush; by trade and investment policies that led to unwieldy
       dollar surpluses in the hands of China and other Asian nations;
       and by tax policies and anti-union business practices that wid-
       ened economic inequality and led to the need to prop up con-
       sumer demand through the accumulation of debt.

       The financial crisis became widely visible in September
       2008 when the New York investment bank Lehman Brothers
       had to close its doors. The crash helped elect Barack Obama
       and a Democratic Congress. Obama's majority reflected the
       growth and increased Democratic commitment of the peculiar
       coalition that had backed McGovern in 1972. These included
       minorities, who were making up a growing percentage of the
       electorate, single women, and professionals. It appeared at the
       time that by responding forcefully to the crash, Obama might
       be able, like Roosevelt in 1933, to create a new enduring Demo-
       cratic majority. But it was not to be. There was a dramatic differ-
       ence from the start: While Roosevelt had been pushed by Long
       and the labor movement from the left, Obama almost immedi-
       ately felt pressure from a new populist movement on the right.

       Obama may have contributed to the public turning right-
       ward. While Roosevelt went after the "moneychangers" during
       his first months in office, Obama's rhetoric and initiatives
       reflected a deference toward Wall Street and the free market. In
       his inaugural address, he cast blame equally on Wall Street and
       Main Street for the crisis. "Our economy is badly weakened, a

consequence of greed and irresponsibility on the part of some, but also our collective failure to make hard choices and prepare the nation for a new age," he declared. Obama's Justice Department did not prosecute or even single out any of the major players in the financial crisis. And on the advice of his Treasury Secretary Timothy Geithner, Obama delayed introducing specific financial reform measures during his first months in office for fear they would shake business confidence. He also gave bailing out the banks priority over aiding insolvent homeowners. That approach would later spark a reaction from the left, but in the first year of Obama's presidency, it left a political vacuum that was filled by the angry right.

The right reacted in particular to initiatives that Obama undertook in his first year. First, he championed several measures to combat the recession. These included a $787 billion stimulus bill and a $75 billion bill to help homeowners threatened by foreclosure. Second, he introduced his plan for national health insurance. To win the support of insurance and drug companies, Obama cobbled together a complex plan that would mandate individuals not covered by their employers to buy insurance from exchanges; the plan would subsidize uninsured lower-income individuals who might not be able to afford insurance on the exchanges. Typical of post-New Deal Democratic social policy, it clearly addressed the needs of lower-income groups, but didn't appear to offer as much to the middle class or, in this case, to senior citizens, who were informed that the plan would be financed by reductions in the growth of Medicare spending.

The reaction spawned the Tea Party movement, which attacked neoliberalism from the far right. The movement was sparked by CNBC commentator Rick Santelli's denunciation of Obama's mortgage plan. "This is America," Santelli, speaking

56   from the floor of the Chicago Mercantile Exchange, exclaimed. "How many of you people want to pay for your neighbor's mortgage that has an extra bathroom and can't pay their bills?" Santelli called for a "Chicago Tea Party" to protest the administration's plan. Santelli's plea was answered by a group of bloggers, policy wonks, and Washington politicos who organized Tea Party protests in February in 30 cities and then more protests in April and September.

The Tea Party has never been a single unified organization. Instead, it consisted of myriad local groups that were independent of each other but united by social media. There were several national Tea Party groups that used their mailing lists to raise money and boost candidates, and two corporate-funded Washington groups, FreedomWorks and Americans for Prosperity, which exploited the movement to further their own lobbying agenda. Sociologists Theda Skocpol and Vanessa Williamson estimated that in 2011, when the movement was probably at its height, Tea Party groups boasted 160,000 members. That doesn't include several million people who during Obama's first term took their cues from what they understood the Tea Party to be advocating. That helped nominate a score of "Tea Party candidates" for the House and Senate in 2010.

There was never a common platform for the Tea Party groups, but there was a certain argument that ran through many of the groups' positions. Santelli expressed it in his rant: the idea that America is divided into "makers" and "takers"— people who earn a living and pay taxes and people who live off of what other people earn. The Tea Party activists viewed Obama's stimulus package and mortgage relief through that prism. They saw themselves as having to pay higher taxes in order to cover for other people's mistakes in buying mortgages they couldn't afford. The Tea Party position was summed up in a bumper sticker that read, "You are not entitled to what I have earned."

The Tea Party also viewed the Affordable Care Act that Congress passed in 2010 as a program aimed at getting people who already had insurance to pay higher premiums and co-payments, so that those who didn't have insurance could afford it. Seniors on Medicare, who had paid for their insurance, would also see their benefits reduced in order to cover the cost of the Affordable Care Act. Emily Ekins, who did extensive interviews with Tea Party members, writes that the Tea Partiers "tended to view the ACA as a redistributive transfer program that they would be disproportionately responsible for funding." Tea Partiers viewed illegal immigration the same way. In their interviews, Skocpol and Williamson report, "the major concern was the illegitimate and costly use of government funds and services by illegal immigrants."

Many of the local Tea Party groups were part of the tradition of American populism and reflected opposition from the right to the neoliberal consensus. They objected to the residual elements of New Deal liberalism that neoliberalism had retained, even those popular among Republicans. If anything, they were a throwback to the Jacksonian proto-populists. The Tea Partiers' argument about "makers" and "takers" recalled the "producerism" of the Jacksonians and the People's Party, which was rooted in a distinction between productive and unproductive elements of society. Bankers, land speculators, and gamblers were typically numbered among the unproductive—as were, for the populists, recent immigrants who took jobs from native-born Americans.

The Tea Partiers initially singled out Obama for coddling the "takers," but after Republicans won the Congress in 2010 but failed to deliver on the Tea Party's non-negotiable demands to

58 repeal Obamacare, the Tea Party focused their ire on the Republican establishment. Tea Party candidates ran against both Senate Majority Leader Mitch McConnell and House Majority Leader Eric Cantor—and in the latter case, won. McConnell and Cantor's sin lay in refusing to go all the way in repudiating even the bare rudiments of the neoliberal consensus between the parties and in failing to block even discussion of immigration reform.

Cantor's sin also lay in being too close to Wall Street and the Business Roundtable. In the primary, Tea Party candidate David Brat said, "All the investment banks in New York and D.C.—those guys should have gone to jail. Instead of going to jail, they went on Eric's Rolodex, and they are sending him big checks." This side of the Tea Party, which echoes the original People's Party, was largely ignored by political scientists and other commentators, even after Trump's presidential campaign brought it to the surface.

The right wing's success during Obama's first term was in marked contrast to its relative obscurity during Roosevelt's first term. In the 1930s, there was rightwing opposition to the New Deal led by the Liberty Lobby, but it amounted to a footnote compared to Long and the labor movement on the left. Part of the reason for this was the difference between the political economy of the Great Depression and the Great Recession. During the Great Depression, unemployment climbed as high as 25 percent, and threatened the middle as well as the lower classes. The middle-class voters who looked to Long feared "being plunged back into what they viewed as an abyss of powerlessness and dependence." They didn't scorn those below them, but identified with them.

During the Great Recession, most Americans enjoyed the protections created by the New Deal and Great Society. They didn't have to fear actual starvation, homelessness, and having their savings wiped out in a bank crash. The recession far less affected the older, white middle classes, who formed the base of the Tea Party movement than it did the lower classes. During the Great Recession, the middle class, defined as the third quintile in income statistics, lost pre-tax income, but when post-tax and transfer payments are included, didn't lose income from 2007 through 2011. Unemployment rates were also far higher for those with only a high school education or less than for those with some college or a bachelor's degree. That created a situation in which what parts of the middle class feared most was having to subsidize through higher taxes or healthcare premiums those in the lower classes or illegal and recent legal immigrants. It encouraged a rightwing rather than a leftwing response to the Great Recession and to neoliberalism. A populist response would eventually come from the left, but it would not initially be as widespread or emanate from the same part of the electorate.

Occupy Wall Street

By February 2011, Obama had come under attack from the left for not moving aggressively against Wall Street. That month, a website, AmpedStatus.com, published a report on the American economy entitled, "The Economic Elite vs. the People of the United States." Its author David DeGraw wrote, "It's time for 99 percent of Americans to mobilize and aggressively move on common sense political reforms. It has now become evident to a critical mass that the Republican and Democratic parties ... have been bought off by a well-organized Economic Elite who are tactically destroying our way of life." When the Amped-Status site was mysteriously knocked off line, the hacker group Anonymous helped create a new site, and it joined with Amped-Status to form a new effort called A99.

60   A99 called for an occupation of Zuccotti Park near Wall Street on June 14. The demonstration fizzled, but the organizers got together with another group, the New York City General Assembly, that had been protesting city budget cuts and wanted to organize an occupation for the fall. A month later, a Canadian anti-capitalist publication *Adbusters*, citing the success of the Egyptian demonstrations in Tahrir Square, put out a call on its blog for an occupation on September 17 that would "set up tents, kitchens, peaceful barricades and occupy Wall Street for a few months." While *Adbusters* billed itself as anti-capitalist, it rejected defining the occupation's goal as "the overthrow of capitalism" for fear that it "will quickly fizzle into another inconsequential ultra-left spectacle soon forgotten." It suggested coming up with "a deceptively simple Trojan Horse demand . . . that is impossible for President Obama to ignore."

The organizers failed to come up with a single demand—there seemed to be too many of them, most of which demanded an end to the reign of neoliberalism—but on a new Occupy Wall Street website, they came up with a simple slogan, borrowed from the original AmpedStatus post, "We are the 99 percent that will no longer tolerate the greed and corruption of the 1 percent." That slogan, which framed the protest in populist terms, defined the movement as an attack on growing political and economic inequality. On September 17, somewhere over a thousand demonstrators showed up and about 300 ended up camping out on Zuccotti Park. And over the next month—aided by police overreaction—the occupation and the demonstrations it spawned attracted thousands in New York. New occupy movements sprung up in scores of American cities. Occupy Boston, Chicago, Oakland, Los Angeles, and Washington, D.C., to be sure, but also Occupy Tupelo, Wichita, Tampa, Nashville, Missoula, Birmingham, El Paso, and many other cities and towns. It drew primarily from the college-educated young (reducing or writing off student debts was a prominent demand), but also from veterans of past anti-globalization struggles, like the demonstrations in Seattle in 1999 against the World Trade Organization.

Part of the key to Occupy's initial success was that it struck a popular nerve that went well beyond the demonstrators. It exposed the fallacy of neoliberalism's claim to "lift all boats." In his book, *Occupy Nation*, sociologist Todd Gitlin wrote, "Unlike any other movement on the American left in at least three-quarters of a century, this movement began with a majority base of support. . . . What it stood for—economic justice and curbs on the wealthy—was popular." But the movement's rejection of formal leadership, and as the months went on, the reversion to obnoxiously disruptive tactics that affected more than the movement's overt targets, finally undid it. When New York Mayor Michael Bloomberg cleared Zuccotti Park of occupiers on November 15, the movement dissipated and, except for a few web pages, disappeared as an organized force.

But Occupy Wall Street's symbolic impact was huge. It brought the issue of political and economic inequality, an issue that lay at the heart of the challenge to neoliberalism, to the fore—not just in the United States, but in Europe, where populist parties in Greece and Spain were inspired by the movement's example. Micah White, the American senior editor of *Adbusters* who helped inspire the movement, called it a "constructive failure." In the 2012 election, Obama borrowed from Occupy Wall Street's rhetoric to pillory Republican Mitt Romney. And Occupy's radicalism would recur in more organized form—when a Vermont senator would decide to run for president in 2016.

The Silent Majority and the Political Revolution: Donald Trump and Bernie Sanders

In an interview with the *Washington Post* in July 2015, former Maryland Governor Martin O'Malley dismissed Bernie Sanders as a "protest candidate." "I'm not running for protest candidate, I'm running for President of the United States," O'Malley declared. But after receiving 0.57 percent of the vote in the Iowa Caucus on February 2, O'Malley dropped out, while Sanders, who tied Clinton in Iowa, moved on to New Hampshire, where he won the primary easily and established himself as a viable contender for the nomination.

Donald Trump's candidacy was also greeted with derision. Two weeks after O'Malley dismissed Sanders's candidacy, the Huffington Post's Washington editors announced that they wouldn't "report on Trump's campaign as part of the Huffington Post's political coverage. Instead, we will cover his campaign as part of our entertainment section. Our reason is simple: Trump's campaign is a sideshow." Six months later, with Trump leading the Republican pack in the polls, Huffington Post editor Ariana Huffington sheepishly announced they were moving their coverage of him back into their politics section.

Many political experts attributed the candidates' success to
something other than what they were advocating. Trump's coalition, the *New York Times* wrote, "is constructed around personality not substance." Sanders's success was attributed to his "authenticity." A column in Politico asked why Sanders's young supporters "are so obsessed with Sanders's authenticity?"

Part of the candidates' appeal did lie with their personal style. Sanders, the 74-year-old democratic socialist, exuded a passion and sincerity that appeared to be lacking in Hillary Clinton's campaigning. As a man of the turbulent '60s, when the young were unwilling to accept the status quo, he was able to establish an emotional bond with young voters. And Trump, a seasoned television performer, had the rare skill of saying virtually the same thing to one audience after another but appearing each time to be having a conversation with his audience. His was in marked contrast to the wooden style of his chief rival, former Florida Governor Jeb Bush.

But over the decades, there has been no absence of candidates who appear authentic, but who haven't fared as well as Sanders. They include Iowa Senator Tom Harkin and former Vermont Governor Howard Dean on the Democratic side and former Pennsylvania Senator Rick Santorum and former Congressman Jack Kemp among the Republicans. Equally, there have been Republicans like Pat Robertson or Pat Buchanan and Democrats like Jesse Jackson who could entertain and enliven an audience as effectively as Trump, but who never got as far as Trump did.

What's missing from these explanations is the way Trump's and Sanders's political messages have resonated with large parts of the electorate. From the right and left, respectively, Trump and Sanders were taking aim at the neoliberal consensus, to which many voters, without naming or identifying it as such,

64   have become hostile, particularly in the wake of the Great
      Recession. Trump and Sanders were continuing what Perot and
      Buchanan had started, but with a success that suggested the
      political consensus had become increasingly vulnerable.

Trump and Neoliberalism

Trump was the son of a real estate developer from Queens who
had made a small fortune building and renting out low- and
middle-income apartments in the borough. Donald Trump
aspired to more—he wanted the wealth and prestige from
building and living in Manhattan. Trump eventually developed a billion dollar business out of hotels, apartment buildings, casinos, and other properties. He also gained the celebrity
he sought. In 1981, when Trump was only 35, he was featured in
People magazine. He joined exclusive clubs frequented by sport
stars, gangsters, and other nouveaux riches. He almost went
under in the 1990s as his investments in Atlantic City casinos
floundered, but he recouped his losses and became a television
star with his own show, *The Apprentice*.

Real estate developers like Trump need licenses and sometimes contracts from cities and states, and have to be perpetu-
ally wooing politicians. He courted and funded Democrats as
well as Republicans, and for his first decades in business, kept
his political opinions largely to himself. But under the tute-
lage of Republican operative Roger Stone, who after Roy Cohn's
death in 1986, became Trump's *consigliere*, Trump began to
dabble in national politics. In 1987, he ran a full-page ad in *The
New York Times* and other major dailies titled "There's nothing
wrong with America's foreign defense policy that a little back-
bone can't cure." In October that year at the invitation of a New
Hampshire Republican who wanted to draft him for president,
he aired his views on defense, trade, and business at a Rotary

Club luncheon in Hampton, New Hampshire. Trump attracted a
larger crowd than any of the announced Republican candidates,
but he demurred from running.

In 1999, Trump actively sought the nomination of the
Reform Party, which Ross Perot had created as a vehicle for his
second presidential run in 1996. Stone formed an exploratory
committee for him, but Trump backed out after several months
and ceded the nomination to Pat Buchanan. In 2011, he again
hinted at interest in the Republican nomination; after Mitt
Romney's loss, Trump began preparing for the 2016 race with
appearances in Iowa the next year and at the Conservative Political Action Conference in Washington.

Trump's views, as expressed over these two decades, defy
easy categorization. On the issues which Democrats and Republicans normally battle over, such as abortion and gay rights and
social spending, Trump, like Stone, was a moderate Eastern
Republican similar, say, to former Republican Senator Alfonse
D'Amato or even Democrat Ed Koch. He supported abortion
rights ("I'm very pro-choice," Trump declared in 1999), he
wanted to protect Social Security and Medicare from cuts, and
he even backed some kind of universal national health insurance.
"I'm a conservative on most issues, but a liberal on health," he
wrote in his 2000 campaign manifesto, *The America We Deserve*.
As a real estate developer, he enthusiastically favored infrastructure spending that many conservative Republicans disdained.

In the 2016 campaign, he abandoned his support for abortion rights, a political necessity in Republican primaries. But he
retained his defense of Social Security and Medicare and even
suggested—without spelling out a plausible program—that he
would replace the Affordable Care Act with a program for universal health insurance. He also backed massive expenditures
on highways, bridges, and airports.

66   If he had based his campaign on this moderate Republicanism, Trump probably would not have won a single delegate. He would have suffered the same fate as Howard Baker, Lamar Alexander, Jon Huntsman, and other centrist candidates. But he combined his moderate Republicanism with a set of convictions, most of which went back two decades or more, that were very similar to those of Perot or Buchanan. They challenged the prevailing Democratic and Republican views of foreign policy, trade and investment, and immigration. They formed the substance of his campaign:

Defense and national security: As the Cold War ended, leading Republicans and Democrats had sought to maintain the alliance system forged during the Cold War and to support American military intervention abroad to sustain the American-led system. In his first public statement of his views in 1987, Trump insisted that the United States get Japan, Saudi Arabia, and other allies to pay for the protection they were getting from the U.S. The United States, Trump wrote, "should stop paying to defend countries that can afford to defend themselves." Trump wanted the country free to devote its resources at home to "our farmers, our sick, our homeless." In the 2016 campaign, he would return to the same point. "You have countries in NATO that are getting a free ride," Trump complained on CNN. "It's very unfair. The United States cannot afford to be the policeman of the world anymore, folks. We have to rebuild our own country."

     Like Perot and Buchanan, Trump went from insisting on "burden sharing" to questioning America's Cold War commitment to NATO and to other alliances. In his 2016 campaign, he criticized NATO as "obsolete" and "expensive." Trump also opposed American military intervention when there was not a direct threat posed to the United States. Perot and Buchanan

had both rejected George H. W. Bush's intervention in Kuwait.
Trump criticized George W. Bush's invasion of Iraq. Trump
insisted that his skills as a dealmaker could improve American
diplomacy. Unlike his opponents in 2016, he didn't promise
to tear up the Obama administration's agreement with Iran.
Instead, he said he would "police that deal." While he promised to destroy ISIS, he suggested that he could make a deal with
Russian President Vladimir Putin, whom he admired, to end the
Syrian conflict. Taken together, Trump's views, like those of
Perot, represented a version of foreign policy realism that was
contrary to both Republican neo-conservatism and Democratic
liberal interventionism.

Free trade: Along with Buchanan and Perot, Trump opposed
NAFTA and the pre-WTO most-favored-nation trading status
for China. He claimed these agreements cost American jobs by
incurring trade deficits. Other countries, he said in 1999, "can't
believe how easy it is to deal with the U.S. We are known as a
bunch of saps. We need our best people to negotiate against the
Japanese and many other countries." Trump promised to get
business leaders to negotiate these treaties.

In his 2016 campaign, Trump opposed the Trans-Pacific
Partnership agreement that the Obama administration had
signed, but Congress had not ratified. And Trump continued to
rail against trade arrangements with China, Japan, and Mexico,
with China drawing the most ire. "Our country is in serious
trouble. We don't win anymore. We don't beat China in trade.
We don't beat Japan, with their millions and millions of cars
coming into this country, in trade. We can't beat Mexico, at
the border or in trade," Trump declared in the first Republican
debate in August 2015. To force China to revalue its currency
to make its exports more expensive, and American exports to

China cheaper, Trump proposed threatening them with a 45 percent tariff on their exports to the United States. And he reiterated his promise to have businessmen and not "political hacks" negotiate trade deals.

Outsourcing and offshoring: In 1999, Trump's principal case against trade treaties was that they allowed foreign countries to keep out American goods while sending their own goods to the United States. But beginning with his 2011 manifesto, *Time to Get Tough*, Trump, like Perot and Buchanan, began to criticize American corporations for taking advantage of trade treaties to outsource their production to Mexico, China, and Japan and to establish factories in these countries that would export goods back to the United States, in both cases depriving American workers of jobs. In *Time to Get Tough*, he proposed a 15 percent tariff on goods that were outsourced.

In the 2016 campaign, Trump singled out specific corporations for shipping or planning to ship factories and jobs either south of the border or overseas. In his announcement speech in July 2015, he dwelled on the example of Ford saying it was going to build a $2.5 billion car and truck plant in Mexico. Trump said that if he were president, he would call the CEO of Ford and threaten him with a 35 percent tax on every car and truck that Ford shipped across the border. Trump also criticized Nabisco for planning to move its plant from Illinois. "They are moving their plant to Mexico. Why, how does it help us?" Trump asked during a speech in Dallas in September 2015. And in the Republican primary debate in February 2016, he went after Carrier for moving a plant and 1,400 jobs from Indianapolis to Mexico. "In the old days, they moved from New York to Texas," Trump said. "Now they go from this country to another country, finding lower labor and lower taxes, they have no real loyalty to the United States."

Like Perot, Trump wanted to restore American manufacturing—it was central to his promise to make America great again. Trump increasingly used the same language as Perot. Speaking in New York after his primary victory April 19, he said, "Our jobs are being sucked out of our state. They're being sucked out of our country, and we're not going to let that happen anymore." Liberal commentators and economists charged that Trump was deceiving the public by promising to bring back jobs that could never be restored. That was probably true. But Trump was taking aim at the skewed distribution of jobs and income that neoliberal economics had created over the prior decades.

Trump also denounced corporate plans—dubbed "tax inversions"—by which corporations moved their headquarters overseas in order to avoid paying American taxes. Trump made these criticisms of corporate offshoring and outsourcing and tax inversions in every speech of his that I heard. Together, these stands struck at the heart of the neoliberal agenda. And in June, after he sewed up the Republican nomination and turned his attention to the general election, he began reemphasizing these themes in his speeches. In a June 22 speech on "The Stakes of this Election," Trump asked "Bernie Sanders's voters to join our movement: so together we can fix the system for *all* Americans. Importantly, this includes fixing all of our many disastrous trade deals. Because it's not just the political system that's rigged. It's the whole economy. It's rigged by big donors who want to keep down wages. It's rigged by big businesses who want to leave our country, fire our workers, and sell their products back into the U.S. with absolutely no consequences for them. . . . It's rigged against you, the American people."

Immigration: When Trump was seeking the Reform Party nomination in 1999, he agreed with Buchanan, his rival for the

70   nomination, on only two issues, trade and immigration. In his campaign book, he wrote:

> America is experiencing serious social and economic difficulty with illegal immigrants who are flooding across our borders. We simply can't absorb them. . . . The majority of legal immigrants can often make significant contributions to our society because they have special skills and because they add to our nation's cultural diversity. . . . But legal immigrants do not and should not enter easily. It's a long, costly, draining, and often frustrating experience—by design. . . . It comes down to this: We must take care of our own people first. Our policy to people born elsewhere should be clear: Enter by the law, or leave.

Trump did not waver from this stance over the next 16 years. In his 2011 book, he wrote, "Illegal immigration is a wrecking ball aimed at U.S. taxpayers. Washington needs to get tough and fight for 'We the People,' not for the special interests who want cheap labor and a minority voting bloc." In the 2016 campaign, he not only opposed illegal immigration, but favored deportation. His case against illegal immigration was partly economic—they drove down wages and raised social costs—but also socio-cultural—they were a cause of crime. He proposed that Mexico finance a wall with its trade surplus from the United States to stop illegal immigration.

Trump's views on immigration displayed a special animus toward Mexican Americans. Trump described Mexico as sending America people who bring "crime" and "drugs" and who are "rapists." He described a judge in a lawsuit brought against Trump University as a "Mexican," even though he was born in Indiana, and called for him to step down from the case. Trump's view recalled the nineteenth-century nativists of the Know-Nothing Party and the People's Party support for deporting

Chinese laborers. But where the People's Party's racist or xenophobic views of the Chinese were secondary to the thrust of
their populism, Trump's views of Mexicans—as well as of
Muslim immigrants—became increasingly central to his appeal.

The Silent Majority

On the surface, Trump appeared to be an unlikely candidate for
a populist campaign. He was, after all, a billionaire who flaunted
his wealth. But Tom Watson had also been a wealthy landowner
and Ross Perot was also a billionaire. What's important is that
Trump, like the Texarkana-born Perot, wasn't a perfect fit for
upper class America. He was still the boy from Queens who
aspired to live on the Upper East Side, but ended up spending
his time at demimonde hangouts like Studio 54 rather than the
Harvard Club.

Trump's view of his social class was also influenced by
Roger Stone. Stone had gotten his start in politics doing dirty
tricks for Nixon's 1972 campaign. Like Trump, he was a moderate Republican on issues like abortion and social spending—
he and his first wife founded Republicans for Choice—but he
liked to frame campaigns in frankly populist terms of "we the
people" vs. the special interests. Trump's biographer Michael
D'Antonio writes of Stone:

> In general, Stone's attacks were intended to persuade voters
> that the GOP, which was traditionally the party of big business
> and the country-club set, was actually the anti-elite party of
> the working class.

Trump took this tack in his campaigns. In an op-ed in *The New
York Times* in February 2000, Trump explained that he was
abandoning his presidential bid because he no longer saw the
Reform Party as a viable vehicle. But he said he regretted not

72   being able to run "a race against Mr. Bush and Mr. Gore, two establishment politicians." "I felt confident," he wrote, "that my argument that America was being ripped off by our major trade partners and that it was time for tougher trade negotiations would have resonance in a race against the two Ivy League contenders." (Trump failed to note that he had graduated from an Ivy League university.)

In 2016, he portrayed himself as the champion of the "silent majority"—a term borrowed from Nixon—against the "special interests" and the "establishment" of both parties. "The silent majority is back, and it's not silent. It's aggressive," Trump declared in Dallas. At rallies, the campaign gave out signs, "The silent majority stands with Trump." In January right before the Iowa caucuses, Trump ran an ad titled "The Establishment." Seated behind a desk, he said, "The establishment, the media, the special interest, the lobbyists, the donors, they're all against me. I'm self-funding my campaign. I don't owe anybody anything. I only owe it to the American people to do a great job. They are really trying to stop me."

Some of Trump's demands reflected his own peculiar brand of salesmanship. In *The Art of the Deal*, Trump explained that a "little hyperbole" helped sell products. And in this sense, a proposal to ban *all* Muslims or to slap a 45 percent tariff on Chinese imports or to get Mexico to pay for a wall may have been deliberate attention-getting ploys, not to be taken seriously. But they were also typical of a populist approach. They were his equivalent of "free silver" or Long's confiscatory tax on the wealthy—incapable of being negotiated, even by the great dealmaker, but just for that reason dramatizing the difference between what the "silent majority" wanted and what the "establishment" would condone. Trump's supporters didn't necessarily believe that he could get Mexico to pay for a wall or that he could deport all immigrants who had entered the country illegally. What they heard in his demand was a point of demarcation between what "we" wanted and what "they"—Congress, the Mexican president—would accept.

Some of Trump's demands about trade and runaway shops and his tirades against lobbyists, big donors, and special interests recalled Perot, but Trump conducted himself much differently from Perot. Perot's manner was professorial and at worst condescending—he was widely and unfairly criticized for referring to an NAACP audience as "you people"—but he was not nasty toward those who disagreed with him and didn't scapegoat out groups. Trump was highly personal in his attacks on rivals and bigoted in his characterizations of nationalities and religions and demeaning in his attitude toward women. (When Hillary Clinton declared her candidacy Trump tweeted, "If Hillary Clinton can't satisfy her husband what makes her think she can satisfy America?")

While Trump's views most clearly echoed the rightwing populism of Wallace and Buchanan, his manner was different from those men as well. Wallace studiously avoided appearing bigoted toward blacks. He almost always couched his proposals in terms of state's rights or some other abstract principle. And unlike Trump, Wallace was an experienced professional politician. He enjoying sparring with critics and protestors at his rallies. By contrast, Trump repeatedly displayed the thin skin of a businessman who treasured his celebrity. At his rallies, he cheered supporters who beat up protestors. And he tried to turn his supporters against the press. Trump's actions reflected a bilious disposition, a meanness borne out of bare-knuckle real estate and casino squabbles—in 1993 Trump tried to repeal a law allowing destitute Indian tribes to operate casinos—and a conviction, borne out of his financial success or, perhaps,

74   arrested development, that he could say in public whatever he thought in private about Mexicans or women without suffering any consequences.

Stone himself formally left as the campaign's head in August 2015 after Trump excoriated Fox News commentator Megyn Kelly, although Stone remained a supporter and advisor. From Stone's standpoint, Trump's nastiness detracted from his anti-establishment message. But Trump continued to climb in the polls. He may in the end have tossed away any chance of being President, but his nastiness—seen as defying standards of political correctness—combined with his substantive appeals on trade, immigration, and runaway shops, tapped into a vein of support among Republicans and independents.

Trump and the Republicans

Trump's success threatened the coalition that conservative Republicans had forged in the 1970s. That coalition included the party's business interests and white working- and middle-class voters who had begun fleeing the Democratic Party in the 1960s. Trump's candidacy drove a wedge into that coalition. Trump's stands against neoliberal economics and neo-conservative foreign policy deeply offended the party's upper crust of business leaders, think tankers, writers, editors, columnists, and television and radio hosts. These leaders waged a vigorous and unsuccessful multi-million dollar campaign against his candidacy. Their real target was often Trump's positions on the economy and foreign policy. After Trump's tirade against multinationals and trade deals in his June speech on "the Stakes" of the election, top Republican donor Paul Singer warned that if Trump were elected, it would cause "a widespread global depression." But Trump's intemperance and bigotry allowed them to condemn him on other counts without emphasizing

their substantive concerns with his foreign and domestic economic views.

Trump's political base was among the party's white
working- and middle-class voters—precisely the voters who
had originally flocked to Wallace and then to Nixon, who had
been attracted by Perot and Buchanan, but who now felt that
they had found a champion in Trump. He had become the voice
of middle American radicalism and more broadly of the white
Americans who felt left behind by globalization and the shift to
a post-industrial economy. There have been two extensive polls
of Republican voters: the first by the American National Election Studies (ANES) in January 2016 and the second by the Pew
Research Center in March. They bear out the same conclusions
about Trump's supporters.

Trump's supporters were older and disproportionately less
educated—the surest sign of class standing—than those of the
other candidates. In 1971, when Donald Warren surveyed Wallace voters, a working-class voter could be assumed to have no
more than a high school education. By 2016, these voters might
have gone to junior college or a trade school and have an associ-
ate's degree. By that standard, 70.1 percent of Trump voters in
the ANES survey were not college graduates, compared to 45.1
of Republican establishment favorite John Kasich's voters. In
income, half of Trump's voters made less than $50,000 a year,
while only 35.3 percent of Kasich's voters made that little. These
Trump voters can be characterized as the descendants of those
white working-class voters who begin leaving the Democrats in
the '60s. Already alienated from Washington and the changes
they had seen around them in 1972, they had become even more
so in 2016, as the Great Recession seemed like the final blow
to their economic prospects in an economy that disproportionately favored the upper middle class and very rich.

Of all the Republican voters, Trump's appear to have been the most worried by the Great Recession, even if they themselves were not thrown out of work. They were the most pessimistic about the economy. According to the Pew poll, 48 percent of Trump voters thought economic conditions in the United States were poor compared to 31 percent of Cruz voters and 28 percent of Kasich voters.

There were also clear differences between Trump's and other Republicans' supporters over immigration and trade. According to the Pew poll, 69 percent of Trump voters thought immigrants did more to burden than to strengthen the country. For Kasich voters, this was 40 percent. According to ANES, 66.4 percent of Trump voters opposed birthright citizenship for immigrant children born in the United States. That was compared to 26 percent of Kasich voters. According to Pew, 67 percent of Trump supporters thought free trade agreements were bad for the United States compared to 46 percent of Kasich supporters and 40 percent of Cruz supporters. Trump voters were also the least likely to think that people should be more sensitive in what they say about people with different backgrounds. According to ANES, 75.7 percent of Trump voters, compared to 45.9 percent of Kasich voters, thought people were too easily offended.

Trump supporters fit the profile of middle American populism. They were skeptical about the powers below *and* above. According to the Pew poll, 61 percent of Trump voters thought that the U.S. economic system unfairly favored the powerful compared to 51 percent of Kasich voters and 45 percent of Cruz supporters. In interviews I conducted at rallies, Trump voters invariably praised his self-financing, which was seen as making him independent of special interests and lobbyists. It was an important part of his appeal, as it was of Perot's.

Trump's voters, like Wallace's, also continued to favor the universal social programs that had originated with the New Deal, while opposing programs like the Affordable Care Act that they thought primarily benefited minorities and the poor. According to the Pew poll, 73 percent of Trump voters opposed any reduction in Social Security. Trump's voters were economic populists; they were not free market libertarians like many of the wealthy backers of groups like the Club for Growth or Free-domWorks; and they were also not hardline social conservatives who put a candidate's stand on prayer or abortion first and who were willing to go along with the Republican business agenda.

Trump appeared aware that he was threatening the Republican coalition. In an interview with Bloomberg News, he said, "Five, ten years from now—different party. You're going to have a worker's party. A party of people that haven't had a real wage increase in eighteen years, that are angry." Would this actually happen? Would a party that had represented corporate and small business America since at least 1896 turn its back on its longstanding constituency? His immediate impact may be limited by the way he conducted his general election campaign. Like a businessman who having succeeded in introducing a new product refuses to recognize that his market has changed, Trump continued after June the same impromptu assaults on his rival and the press and the same casual bigotry that had won him the Republican nomination. That could lead to a defeat that will cast a temporary pall on the substance of his populism. Trump's longer-term influence may also be limited by his having been, like Long, Wallace, and Perot, the singularly charismatic messenger for his populism. But his candidacy will have produced another crack in the neoliberal firmament.

Sanders and the Billionaire Class

Sanders, like Trump, was raised in one of New York's outer boroughs, but the resemblance ends there. Sanders grew up in Brooklyn in humble circumstances. His father was a Jewish émigré from Poland who sold paint and his mother the daughter of émigrés. He went to the same high school that Ruth Bader Ginsburg and Chuck Schumer attended, and he spent a year at Brooklyn College before transferring to the University of Chicago, where he graduated in 1964. He lived on a Kibbutz in Israel for six months, returned to New York where he worked at odd jobs, and in 1968, he and his first wife moved to Vermont as part of the New Left's back-to-the-land movement.

The Brooklyn in which Sanders grew up was a hotbed of leftwing politics and culture, and Sanders, when he came to Chicago, joined the Young People's Socialist League, the youth wing of Norman Thomas's Socialist Party, and the Congress of Racial Equality (CORE), which at the time was a militant civil rights group. He read Marx and the history of American socialism, and got arrested in civil rights protests, but he never took the turn toward sectarian violence the leaders of SDS (Students for a Democratic Society) took in the late '60s. Instead, Sanders combined a commitment to the socialism of Eugene Debs with various counterculture enthusiasms, including free love, Reichian therapy, ecology, home birth, and home schooling.

Living on odd jobs while raising a young child, Sanders ran for Senate twice and governor twice in the '70s on the ticket of the Liberty Union, a leftwing third party in Vermont. Disillusioned—he got no more than 6 percent of the vote—he quit the Liberty Union in 1977. Four years later, he ran for mayor of Burlington, and to the surprise of the town's leaders, won by 10 votes over the Democratic incumbent. Sanders was a successful mayor. He was reelected three times and helped turn the town of 45,000 into one of New England's most livable cities. In 1990, he won Vermont's seat in the House of Representatives, and in 2006, when Republican Jim Jeffords retired, Sanders won one of the Senate seats.

In his Liberty Union campaigns, Sanders advocated for socialism. In the diary he kept of his Senate campaign in 1972, he wrote of a campaign stop, "I even mentioned the horrible word 'socialism'—and nobody in the audience fainted." He would recommend Albert Einstein's essay, "Why Socialism," to anyone interested. In that essay, Einstein wrote that the only way to remove the "evils" of capitalism was "through the establishment of a socialist economy. . . . In such an economy, the means of production are owned by society itself and are utilized in a planned fashion." As mayor, Sanders fretted that he couldn't bring socialism to Vermont. "If you ask me if the banks should be nationalized, I would say yes," Sanders told the *Baltimore Sun*. "But I don't have the power to nationalize the banks in Burlington."

After Sanders was elected to Congress, his view of socialism softened and increasingly came to resemble social democracy. "To me socialism doesn't mean state ownership of everything by any means," he told the AP in November 1990. "It means creating a nation and a world, in which all human beings have a decent standard of living." In his 1997 autobiography, *Outsider in the House*, Sanders did write, "Bill Clinton is a moderate Democrat. I'm a democratic socialist." But in this book he most often describes himself as a "progressive." By the time, he was elected to the Senate, he explicitly equated socialism with Scandinavian social democracy. "I'm a democratic socialist," he told the *Washington Post*. "In Norway, parents get a paid year

80   to care for infants. Finland and Sweden have national health care, free college, affordable housing, and a higher standard of living."

What hadn't changed over the years was Sanders's indictment of capitalism. He still saw yawning economic inequality. In his 1971 campaign, he had called for radical tax reform directed at the "two percent of the people controlling one third of the country's wealth." In his 1996 Senate reelection campaign, he attacked the influence of the "one percent." In the House and Senate, he stood firm against the party's embrace of neoliberalism. He opposed NAFTA and the agreements with China, tax cuts on business, budgets that reduced social spending, and financial deregulation. He continued to dissent in the Obama years. In December 2010—in a move echoing Huey Long's rejection of Roosevelt's Government Economy Act in 1933—he staged a one-man filibuster against the budget and tax agreement that Obama, chastened by congressional losses, had worked out with the Republicans that prolonged the Bush tax cuts for the wealthy.

Sanders first started thinking seriously about running for president in April 2013, when he called a meeting in Burlington with his top friends and advisors to discuss whether he should do so. The group speculated that Sanders's outrage over income inequality might find a ready reception in 2016. They noted that the Occupy Wall Street protests had dissipated, but that the issues they had raised were now widely discussed. Sanders took another two years to make a final decision, but in April 2015, he told his friends he was running. In an interview with Rachel Maddow on MSNBC that month, Sanders, noting "this strange moment in American history, when our middle class is disappearing, when we have so many people living in poverty, when we have to deal with climate change, when we

have to deal with the horrendous level of income and wealth
inequality," asked

> [H]ow do we address these issues in a way that takes on the
> billionaire class. Where they have significant control over the
> media, where they by and large determine the legislation that
> goes on in Congress, and as a result of *Citizens United* are pre-
> pared to buy the United States Congress."

As his campaign unfolded, Sanders unveiled a set of radical
reforms that would, among other things, entail government
reassuming control over the private market. He proposed Medicare for all (which would remove private insurance as a mid-
dleman and guarantee health insurance as a right), free tuition
to public colleges financed by a transaction tax on Wall Street
speculation, a carbon tax to reduce carbon emissions, the rein-
statement of the Glass-Steagall Act separating commercial and
investment banking, and public campaign financing.

Sanders's critics among Democrats argued that his proposals were impractical because they would never get through a
Republican congress. A column in *New York* magazine was entitled, "What Bernie Sanders Doesn't Understand About American Politics." Sanders responded that to obtain any of these
reforms, there would have to be a "political revolution" that
pitted the power of the people against the billionaire class. "If we
are going to transform America," Sanders said during a speech
in North Las Vegas in November, "We need a political revolution. Millions of people have to stand up and get involved in the
political process in a way we have not in many, many years."

In an editorial, *The New York Times* criticized Sanders's
"facile calls for revolution," but what Sanders meant by "revolution" was greater active participation in politics rather than
armed struggle to seize state power. Coupled with his demand

82   for reform of campaign finance, Sanders was actually making a much more arguable point than *The New York Times* and other critics were willing to acknowledge: namely, that to achieve the kind of significant change in the existing relationship between the government and economy that his reforms would entail would require a major shift in political power and allegiance in the country, such as had happened between, say, 1929 and 1935.

In an interview with Stephen Colbert, Sanders said that he would prefer to describe his proposals as "progressive" rather than as "socialist" or "liberal." That use of the term "progressive" made sense, but historically speaking, American progressivism had arisen as an alternative to populism and socialism. Where populism had rested on a conflict between the people and the establishment, and socialism on a conflict between the working class and the capitalist class, progressivism sought to reconcile classes—to remove antagonisms. "'I am for labor,' or 'I am for capital,' substitutes something else for the immutable laws of righteousness," Theodore Roosevelt wrote in 1904. "The one and the other would let the class man in, and letting him in is the one thing that will most quickly eat out the heart of the republic."

Sanders's political approach and his demands fit more appropriately into the American populist tradition of the People's Party, Long, Perot, and Occupy Wall Street. He aimed to rouse the people against the "billionaire class." And his demands created a political divide between the 99 percent and the 1 percent. They defined the conflict rather than providing an opening to negotiations. There was no way that the insurance and drug companies would permit "Medicare for all" without what Sanders called a political revolution, or that the banks and other Wall Street firms would submit to further regulation or pay transaction taxes so that Americans could go to public college for free. In a manner recalling how the political elites dealt with Long and Perot, Sanders's critics argued that his numbers didn't add up, as if the demands in a campaign needed to pass muster at the Congressional Budget Office.

Sanders agreed with Trump about trade treaties and foreign investment. "My understanding, talking to many economists, is that NAFTA, PNTR [permanent normal trade relations] with China, other trade agreements have cost this country millions of jobs," Sanders told the *New York Daily News*. He added, "I don't think it is appropriate for trade policies to say that you can move to a country where wages are abysmal, where there are no environmental regulations, where workers can't form unions." But Sanders was a leftwing and not a rightwing populist. Unlike Trump and his supporters, he didn't blame unauthorized immigrants for the plight of American workers or seek to end terrorism by banning Muslims from coming into the country. He was entirely focused, as he explained to Maddow, on combating the "billionaire class."

The Bernie Voters

In the 2016 election, Sanders lost the battle for the nomination, but the support for Hillary Clinton may not have reflected the extent to which Democrats and Democratic-leaning independents were supportive of his approach. Much of the nominating contest hinged on the belief of African American and older voters that Clinton was more electable in a general election and more prepared, after her years at the highest levels of power, to assume the presidency than the 74-year-old democratic socialist who during the election showed very little interest in or knowledge of foreign policy. But something can still be learned from looking at Sanders's core supporters.

Sanders's support, like Trump's, showed how much the Great Recession had radicalized significant parts of the

84   electorate. Of all voting groups, his voters were the most harshly critical of the American economic system. In the Pew poll, 91 percent of Sanders's voters thought that the "U.S. system unfairly favors the powerful." That's in comparison to 73 percent of Clinton voters and 61 percent of Trump voters. According to Pew, 82 percent of Sanders's voters also thought that corporations "make too much profit." In the ANES poll, 90.2 percent of Sanders's voters thought the differences in income between the rich and poor were larger than they were 20 years ago.

Sanders's voters were also the most pessimistic about their own and the country's economic future. That too shows the impact of the Great Recession. In the Pew survey, 57 percent—far more than any other Democratic or Republican voting bloc—thought that hard work is no guarantee of success. In the ANES survey 63.3 percent of Sanders's supporters (compared to 43.2 percent of Clinton supporters) thought there was either no or little opportunity for the average person to get ahead in America.

On average, Sanders got his greatest support among young people. From my observations at rallies, many of these young voters were either going to college or had recently graduated from college. They are, in effect, the descendants of the McGovern generation who began gravitating to the Democratic party over post-material social and environmental concerns and over moral outrage at the Vietnam War and later the American invasion of Iraq and more recently, in the wake of the Great Recession, what they saw as the irresponsibility of Wall Street and the billionaire class.

But there was also a material dimension to their concern that Sanders touched. They were worried about the opportunities that awaited them, or that they had found, on the job market. They found less autonomy in their work; they made less than they had expected. In the wake of the Great Recession,

these young voters became concerned whether *any* jobs would
await them, and whether they would ever be able to pay back the
debts they had incurred to go to college.

They might, of course, be won over to neoliberal economics
by a reversal of these trends in the economy, but it's not likely
to happen. In the last decades of the twentieth century, economists talked about a college graduate wage premium but it shrunk
after the boom of the late 1990s. According to the Economic
Policy Institute, the real inflation-adjusted wages of young college graduates were 2.5 percent lower in 2015 than they were in
2000. At the same time, student debts—a key issue in the Sanders's campaign—skyrocketed, rising by 84 percent from 2008 to
2014. In addition, graduates of community and four-year colleges
increasingly have to find roles within a labor force divided into
specialized niches that are being continually reshaped by information technology. That has probably contributed to the rising
levels of anxiety that psychologists have found among college
students. If these trends continue, a large number of radicalized
American voters will begin moving through the electorate.

Sanders's identification as a socialist would have certainly
become a handicap in a general election, but there is some indication that it may have helped him among younger voters. In a January 2016 survey by the polling group YouGov, young adults 18
to 29 had a favorable view of socialism by 43 to 26 percent, with
the remainder having no opinion. Democratic voters had a favorable view by 42 to 34 percent. These results—inconceivable 50 or
even 25 years ago—are partly the result of the Cold War's end and
the identification of socialism with European social democracy
rather than with Soviet communism. Some Sanders supporters
that I interviewed cited European social programs. But others,
reminiscent of nineteenth-century Christian socialists, stressed
the cooperative nature of socialism in contrast to capitalism. In

86   either case, younger voters' attraction to socialism is the flip side of their growing disillusionment with capitalism in the wake of the Great Recession.

Younger voters were also not turned off by Sanders's age, nor by his ignorance of pop culture. There was an affinity between Sanders, who had come of age in the raucous sixties, when young people were determined to look beyond the status quo, and his young supporters. While older voters and liberal pundits evaluated Sanders's program by whether they could be included in the president's Fiscal Year 2018 budget, younger voters liked the visionary sweep of Medicare for All and Free Public College. They understood that adopting programs like these couldn't happen within the current "rigged system" and would require a political revolution. The contrast couldn't have been sharper with Clinton's campaign that lacked any visionary component and dwelt entirely on lists of incremental changes.

As Sanders's chances to win the nomination evaporated, some of his ardent supporters planned meetings to turn his campaign into a political movement that would survive the 2016 election. But it is difficult to turn political campaigns into political movements. Movements most often arise around particular issues (abortion, temperance, civil rights, gay marriage, the Vietnam or Iraq wars), and become widespread when they confront an administration that takes an opposing position. George W. Bush's invasion of Iraq helped spur a movement that helped get Obama the nomination and the presidency in 2008, but the movement failed to survive Obama's election. It is even less plausible to expect Sanders's campaign to spawn a movement that could survive the November election, especially if Hillary Clinton were to be elected. (If Trump is elected, that's a different matter, but in that case, a movement on the left can be expected to arise regardless of Sanders.)

Sanders's impact (like Long's) will be most likely be felt in the Democratic Party, where it has already accelerated the turn against neoliberal orthodoxy on finance, trade, and capital mobility, although not necessarily on unskilled immigration and guest workers. Young people are not a functional voting bloc except as students, but Sanders's campaign has revealed the extent to which the Great Recession radicalized the descendants of the McGovern generation of college-educated professionals. They could be a major force in Americans politics for years to come—and one that could eventually seal the doom of the neoliberal orthodoxy.

The Rise of European Populism

In the last decades of the nineteenth century, as the People's Party was erupting on the American scene, Europe was seeing the emergence of Social Democratic parties inspired by Karl Marx's theory of socialism. Over the next 70 years, Europe would see an array of parties on the left, center and right, but it wouldn't see anything resembling American populism until the 1970s. Europeans would call these parties, which only began to flourish in 1990s by the American-derived name. It's "populiste" in French and "populist" in German.

Like the original American People's Party, the European parties operated within the electoral arena and championed the "people" against an "establishment" or "elite." France's National Front represents the "little people" and the "forgotten members" against the "caste." Finland's Finns Party wants "a democracy that rests on the consent of the people and does not emanate from elites or bureaucrats." Spain's Podemos champions the *gente* against the *casta*—the people against the establishment. Italy's Beppe Grillo rails against what he calls the "three destroyers"—journalists, industrialists, and politicians. Geert

Wilders's Freedom Party represents "Henk and Ingrid" against
"the political elite."

The first European parties were rightwing populist. They accused the elites of coddling communists, welfare recipients, or immigrants. As a result, the term "populist" in Europe became used pejoratively by leftwing and centrist politicians and academics. Political scientist Cas Mudde writes, "In the public debate populism is mostly used to denounce a form of politics that uses (a combination of) demagogy, charismatic leadership, or a *Stammtisch* (pub) discourse." A recent study of European populist parties by a reputable think tank was titled, "Exposing the Demagogues." In the last decade, however, leftwing populist parties have arisen in Spain, Greece, and Italy that direct their ire against the establishment in their country or against the European Union headquarters in Brussels.

The main difference between American and European populists is that while American parties and campaigns come and go quickly, some European populist parties have been around for decades. That's primarily because Europe has multi-party systems, and many of the countries have proportional representation that allows smaller parties to maintain a foothold even when they are polling less than 7 percent in elections. (In France, which has a majority system in presidential elections, the National Front (FN) has still been able to win not only local elections, but seats in the European Parliament, which are allotted proportionally.)

The European parties muddled along in the '70s and '80s, but they caught fire in the 1990s for some of the same reasons that American campaigns did. In Europe, in the wake of the downturn during the '70s, a neoliberal outlook replaced one heavily influenced by social democracy and Keynesian economics. The Socialist, Social Democratic, and Labour parties

90   as well as the Christian Democratic, Conservative, and Liberal parties embraced this outlook, and when it failed to create buoyant prosperity, that left an opening for populists. So, too, did the leading parties' commitments to immigration within the EU and asylum from countries in North Africa and the Middle East.

The End of the Boom

Populist politics were largely absent in Western Europe in the three decades after World War II. In those years, Socialist, Social Democratic, and labour parties shared power relatively equitably with Christian Democrats, Tories, Gaullists, and other centrist and center-right parties. In France and Italy, even Communist parties had a subordinate role. The parties and their supporters in business, labor, and the middle classes, eager to avoid the clashes of the 1920s, cooperated to expand social programs. Countries established universal access to healthcare, generous unemployment benefits and family allowances, and free college education. The center and center-right parties held power more often than not, but a politics borne of reform-minded social democracy and Keynesian economics predominated in the same way that New Deal liberalism held sway in the United States even during Republican administrations.

What sustained this social democratic approach was the economic boom. Western Europe benefited from what economist Brad DeLong called a "virtuous circle":

> Trade expansion drove growth, growth drove expanded social insurance programs and real wage levels; expanded social insurance states and real wage levels social peace, social peace allowed inflation to stay low even as output expanded rapidly, rapidly expanding output led to high investment, which further increased

growth and created the preconditions for further expansions of
international trade.

During this period, unemployment rates were impossibly low. The rate was 0.6 percent in West Germany in 1970, 2.2 percent in the UK, and 2.5 percent in France. In France, this era was called *les trente glorieuses,* or 30 glorious years.

But Europe began to suffer a downturn in the early '70s. The principal cause, as in the United States, was a combination of a profit squeeze from a militant labor movement and the development of global overcapacity in key postwar industries like textiles and steel. But in Western Europe, the slowdown was aggravated by the abandonment of capital controls and America's abandonment of a fixed and overvalued currency that had given Europeans a price advantage. The energy price hike that began in 1973 also hit oil-dependent Europe particularly hard. Growth slowed and unemployment rose. Comparing the period 1950 to 1973 with the period from 1973 to 1995, France's average rate of growth fell from 5.1 to 2.7 percent; Germany's from 6.0 to 2.7 percent; and Sweden's from 4.1 to 1.5 percent. During the 1960s, unemployment in Western Europe averaged a lowly 1.6 percent. By the end of the 1970s, unemployment rose to more than 7 percent. In Italy, which had enjoyed 3.2 percent unemployment in 1971, unemployment among 14- to 29-year-olds rose to 17.2 percent by the decade's end.

As the economy slowed, government revenues declined, while social welfare expenditures rose sharply. In 1976, with deficits soaring and balances of payments in arrears, both Great Britain and Italy had to ask for loans from the International Monetary Fund. Throughout Western Europe, governments tried to limit wage increases in the face of inflationary pressures, but faced militant opposition from powerful labor unions. In Italy, a wave

92 of strikes and student demonstrations from 1969 through 1973 forced concessions in wages and social benefits. In Britain, a miners' strike in early 1974 caused the Conservative government to declare a three-day work week to conserve energy. During the boom, wage increases could be absorbed by higher productivity; but during the slowdown and inflation, they only increased pressure on prices, threatening the balance of trade.

All in all, the slowdown undermined social democratic and Keynesian policy. It turned a virtuous circle into a vicious one. Because of rising oil and food prices, deficits meant to stimulate the economy and reduce unemployment could lead to inflation, which in turn could undermine investment and reduce employment. With heightened competition within a global free market, deficits could lead to more demand for imports and to a growing trade deficit, which threatened a country's currency. These pitfalls of the old approach became apparent first in Great Britain and France. The European version of neoliberalism arose out of the experience that these two countries faced.

In the winter of 1978–79, attempts by Labour Prime Minister James Callaghan to limit wage increases led to a wave of strikes, creating what was called the "winter of discontent." Callaghan's failure to halt Britain's combination of inflation and unemployment led to his defeat in 1979 by Tory Margaret Thatcher. Thatcher had broken with her own party's commitment to Keynesianism. She resorted to what came to be called a neoliberal strategy. She focused on increasing the "supply side"—corporate rates of profit—rather than the demand side. By curtailing the money supply, she raised interest rates, which created a deep recession, that in turn reduced the pressure on wages and prices and the demand for imports, forced obsolete firms out of business, and helped bolster profit rates in the firms that survived.

Thatcher also removed regulations on industry and finance,   93
and lowered taxes on business and the wealthy. She privat-
ized some government industries, and attempted to down-
size others. When coal miners resisted massive layoffs in 1984,
Thatcher held out successfully against them, as Ronald Reagan
had done against the air traffic controllers. Over 250,000 jobs
in national industries were lost, but as a result, the remaining
industries became more efficient, and after 1984, the economy
began to slowly pick up. Writes historian Tony Judt, "There is
no doubt that Britain's economic performance *did* improve in
the Thatcher years, after an initial decline from 1979–81."

But as happened in the United States, the distance between
the top earners and those in the middle and bottom widened,
and the middle-income blue-collar worker was threatened with
extinction. During Thatcher's years (when the top income tax
rate dropped from 60 to 40 percent) the top fifth of all earners
increased their share of the nation's income from 36 to 42 percent. Manufacturing, a source of many middle-income jobs, fell
from 18 percent of GDP when she took office to 15 percent when
she left in 1992. The trend toward inequality continued under
Britain's subsequent Labour and Tory governments. By 2010,
manufacturing accounted for 10 percent of GDP, and inequality
had continued to rise.

In France, inflation had climbed to 14 percent by the 1981
presidential election, and 1.5 million were unemployed. That
allowed François Mitterrand to be elected the first Socialist Party
president of the Fifth Republic. Mitterrand tried to develop an
alternative to Thatcher's neoliberalism. Elected in 1981 after a
center-right government had failed to halt France's slide, Mitterrand and his advisors assumed that the downturn had exhausted
itself and that global demand would soon be picking up. With
a parliamentary majority, Mitterrand and the Socialists enacted

94 a huge boost in social spending aimed at redistributing wealth
and fuelling consumer demand, and they undertook extensive
nationalizations to assure that the profits businesses received
were reinvested. If it wasn't socialism, it was a leftwing version
of Charles de Gaulle's command economy.

Mitterrand's policies did boost economic growth. France's
economy grew 2 percent in his first two years, while most of
Europe's economies were in recession. But by the same token,
with the rest of Europe and the United States in recession, the
demand for France's exports lagged well behind French consumers' demands for imports. France's trade deficit almost
doubled during Mitterrand's first year. That created a balance of
payments crisis.

Ordinarily, a country running very large trade deficits can
devalue its currency, which would make its imports more expensive and its exports cheaper. But France feared devaluation. Oil
was priced in dollars, and if France were to devalue its currency,
its oil bills would soar, negating any effect the devaluation would
have on its trade balance. In addition, France, concerned about
its currency being destabilized by floating dollar, had agreed in
1979 to join with West Germany and the four other members
of the European Economic Community in creating a European
Monetary System (EMS) that required maintaining its currency
within a fixed range.

Mitterrand's Minister of Research of Industry, Jean-Pierre
Chevenement, advocated leaving the EMS and letting the Franc
fall. But Mitterrand, who was also under the sway of the "Franc
fort" (strong Franc) as a symbol of France's greatness, decided
instead to go along a similar road as Thatcher. Beginning in
1982, he reduced demand for imports by reducing consumer
demand through cuts in spending and tax increases and by
freezing wages. Unemployment rose from 7.3 percent in 1981 to

10.5 percent in 1985, but inflation slowed and the trade balance
improved, and after falling, growth began to inch up. It wasn't
entirely clear at the time, but Callaghan's failure and Mitterrand's U-turn signaled the end of postwar consensus around
social democracy and Keynesian economics.

Socialist Lionel Jospin, who was prime minister under Mitterrand's successor Jacques Chirac, ended up privatizing more
of the firms that Mitterrand had nationalized and reducing taxes
on the wealthy. After being highly critical during the election of
the EU's growth and stability pact limiting the size of deficits,
Jospin adhered to it. After taking office in Germany in 1999,
Social Democratic Chancellor Gerhard Schröeder oversaw an
agreement between German unions and management in 1999
to hold down wages. In 2003, Schröeder championed the con-
troversial Hartz laws that made it easier for firms to hire and fire
workers. Labour Prime Minister Tony Blair, who took office in
1995, continued Thatcher's policy of deregulating finance and
business. Asked in 2002 what her greatest achievement was,
Thatcher replied, "Tony Blair and New Labour. We forced our
opponents to change their minds."

Some of the Socialist, Social Democratic, and Labour parties succeeded in winning office and even reelection, as Blair did,
but in abandoning their support for an expanding public sector
and for viable manufacturing industries in favor of supporting
free trade, deregulated finance, and a globalized capitalism, they
began to forfeit the loyalty of their working-class constituents.
That, along with the disintegration of the Communist parties in
France and Italy after the fall of the Soviet Union, left an opening
for a new appeal to the working classes. And the opening, particularly for a rightwing populism, was enlarged by an additional
factor—the rapid growth of a non-European immigrant population at the same time job opportunities were no longer plentiful.

96   Immigrants and Islamists

During the boom years, northern European countries, faced with severe labor shortages, began actively recruiting guest workers. In West Germany, there were 95,000 recruited workers in 1956; by 1966, there were 1.3 million. Two million migrant workers came into France from 1946 to 1970, along with 690,000 dependents. Belgium, the Netherlands, Great Britain, Denmark, and Switzerland had similar programs. And in these countries, employers began recruiting workers independently without authorization. Some countries like Sweden opened their borders to any immigrant who wanted to work. And former colonial powers like France encouraged their former subjects to emigrate. By the early 1970s, there were 4.1 million foreign-born workers in Germany; 1 million in Switzerland; and 3.4 million in France.

During this time, there was little anti-immigrant sentiment in Western Europe. The migrants didn't compete with the natives for jobs, and they were seen as temporary residents who would eventually return home. But the situation changed in the 1970s when labor shortages transformed into labor surpluses. Western Europe ended formal recruitment of foreign workers and even offered workers financial incentives to return to their homelands, but that had unexpected consequences. Workers from other European countries tended to return home, while workers from Africa and the Middle East, where economic conditions were worse than those in recession-hammered Europe, stayed and took advantage of the legal opportunity to bring their families to live in Europe, where they reproduced at a higher rate than native Europeans. As a result, the numbers of immigrants continued to rise, and the proportion of those that came from non-European societies did as well. In France, the proportion of

immigrants from the Maghreb region of western North Africa
increased by 16 percentage points from 1968 to 1982.

In the '80s and '90s, a dramatic increase in asylum-seeking refugees from Africa and Asia further swelled the proportions of non-European immigrants—from 75,000 in 1983 to almost 320,000 in 1989. Since then, these numbers have continued to grow. In Denmark, the number of non-European immigrants increased by 268,902, or 520 percent, between 1980 and 2005, making up 90 percent of the total increase of immigrants to Denmark. Where the previous generation of immigrants had often worked in manufacturing, many now found themselves without jobs or taking menial jobs in hotels, restaurants, or in construction. They clustered in downscale communities inside or on the outskirts or Paris, Marseilles, Antwerp, Brussels, Rotterdam, or Copenhagen. Crime became rife in many of these communities, and some of them, largely populated by Muslims, became cut off culturally from native communities.

Fear and anger over the influx of immigrants from non-European countries began to show up in European polling in the early 1990s. In the Eurobarometer polls taken by the European Commission in 1991, 23 percent of respondents from the 12 nations of the European Economic Community thought that their countries should not accept immigrants from countries south of the Mediterranean. In France, it was 33 percent; in Denmark, 25 percent. In France, 56 percent of respondents thought their country had too many immigrants, and 24 percent thought that France should not accept people seeking asylum. There was a pronounced jump even from 1988. In the autumn 1988 survey, 18 percent of respondents in the EC countries had wanted the rights of immigrants restricted; by 1991, it was 33 percent.

According to the first European Social Survey, done in 2002, the main complaints about immigrants (in this order)

98 were that they made crime worse, took out more social bene-fits than they paid for in taxes, and took jobs away from natives. Many European leaders ignored or denigrated these senti-ments. The European Commission that studied attitudes toward immigrants was called "The Commission of Enquiry on Racism and Xenophobia in Europe." Initially, political parties, especially the Socialist and Social Democratic parties, urged acceptance of the immigrants, including immigrants who had entered the countries illegally. That left a political vacuum that the rightwing populist parties filled.

The Populist Right

Many of today's populist organizations in Western Europe can trace their ancestry from the anti-tax groups of the 1970s (which resemble the American anti-tax movement of those same years) and from nationalist organizations with question-able ties to former fascists and Nazis. Jean-Marie Le Pen, the founder of the National Front, got his start in French book-store owner Pierre Poujade's anti-tax movement of the 1950s. The National Front, which Le Pen founded in 1972, combined remnants of Poujade's shopkeepers' movement with critics of France's decolonization, some of whom, like Le Pen, looked back favorably on Vichy France and downplayed the evils of Hit-ler's Germany. During the 1970s, the FN, which was militantly anti-communist and anti-tax, barely counted in the polls. The FN got 0.76 percent in the 1974 presidential election.

The Danish People's Party was a spin-off from the Prog-ress Party, which tax lawyer Mogens Glistrup founded in 1973. Glistrup, who eventually went to jail for tax evasion, called for abolishing the income tax. The party did surprisingly well in the 1970s, but less so in the 1980s when the Liberals and Con-servatives coopted its anti-tax message. It was revived in 1995 when Pia Kjærsgaard split off and formed the People's Party. The Austrian Freedom Party grew out of the postwar League of Independents, which included former Nazis, and advocated the restoration of the German nation. In 1956, it was succeeded by the Freedom Party, which continued (but moderated) the League's German nationalism, and which functioned as a submissive junior partner to the reigning Social Democratic and Christian Democratic parties. Like the other parties it initially combined nationalism with libertarian anti-tax economics.

Then, from roughly the late 1980s through the early 2000s, these and other older parties, as well as some new populist parties that formed, took off and became players in Western European politics. The National Front, which gravitated between 10 and 15 percent in national elections in the 1990s, got 16.8 percent for Le Pen as its presidential candidate in the first round in 2002, knocking Socialist prime minister Lionel Jospin out of the runoff. In its very first national election in 1998, the Danish People's Party got 7 percent. Then in November 2001, it received 13 percent, putting it in third place. The Austrian Freedom Party went from 16.1 percent in 1990 to 26.9 percent in 1999. The Swiss People's Party went from 11.9 percent in 1991 to 22.5 percent in 1999. And the Norwegian Progress Party went from 3.5 percent in 1985 to 13 percent in 1989 to 15.3 percent in 1997, making it Norway's second largest party.

The most immediate factor in the parties' rise was the way they tied themselves to the growing popular disapproval of non-European immigrants and asylum seekers. During the last two decades of the twentieth century, the parties turned their attention from communism and taxes to immigration. In the fall of 1992, the Austrian Freedom Party announced an "Austria First" initiative that included a constitutional amendment declaring Austria a land of non-immigrants. The new

100   Danish People's Party, formed out of the Progress Party in 1995, introduced a ten-point plan that called for repatriating asylum seekers and repealing Social Democratic legislation that had allowed immigrants to vote in local elections after three years. In Norway, the Progress Party, which had earlier been divided over its attitude toward immigration, adopted a hardline stance in the 1997 elections, raising its national vote from 6.3 percent in 1993 to 15.3 percent.

In his study of the European politics of immigration, Christopher Caldwell described the Danish People's Party as "the most immigrant-obsessed party in Europe." Unlike other Western European countries, Denmark largely escaped the downturn that came in the 1970s. Of European countries, it has one of the most generous welfare states, and the least economic inequality. What sparked the backlash to immigration and asylum seeking were socio-cultural rather than strictly economic concerns. Danes weren't worried that immigrants would take their jobs, but that they wouldn't work at all and would become free riders on Denmark's generous welfare system. (Denmark, for instance, grants up to 90 percent of previous salary for four years for workers who lose their jobs.) That concern was partly economic, but more broadly it stemmed from the idea that the Danish welfare state, financed by high taxes, was based on mutual trust among Danish citizens who shared the same values of work and family and who would not take advantage of the Danish state's generosity. As more Muslim immigrants from the Middle East and North Africa entered Denmark, the critics of immigration also raised concerns about crime and religious practices.

Much of the inspiration for the People's Party stand on immigration came from a Lutheran pastor, Søren Krarup. "Between Glistrup and the founding of the People's Party is a gap," Mikael Jalving, a columnist for *Jyllands-Posten* and the author of a book on Krarup, explained. "The gap was taken up by Søren Krarup." Beginning in the 1980s, Krarup argued that Danes had a special culture informed by Lutheranism to which Islam, which he saw as a political movement and not simply a religion, was antithetical. Krarup's crusade against Denmark's immigration policies was sparked by the Danish parliament's passage in 1983 of an Alien Act welcoming refugees who had begun pouring into Europe from the Iran-Iraq war, and who after the act began entering Denmark annually by the thousands rather than hundreds. Krarup denounced the act as "legal suicide" for allowing "the uncontrolled and unconstrained mass migration of Mohammedan and Oriental refugees [who] come through our borders." In 1997, Krarup was invited to address the newly formed People's Party's convention, and in 2001, he was elected to parliament from the party and headed its immigration and naturalization committee.

The People's Party campaigns were incendiary. One campaign poster from 1999 showed a woman with a *burqa*. The text read: "Your Denmark: A multiethnic society with rapes, violence, insecurity, forced marriages, oppressed women, gang crimes." The leading Social Democratic and Liberal parties dismissed the party and its leader Pia Kjærsgaard, who had been a home health aide. In a debate in parliament that year, Social Democratic Prime Minister Poul Nyrup Rasmussen told her, "You are not house-trained," using a word *stuerene* that normally refers to animals who have not learned to urinate in litter boxes.

But Kjærsgaard had the last laugh on Rasmussen. After the September 11, 2001 al Qaeda attack in the United States, concern about Islamic immigrants rose in Europe. In that November's election, which was dominated by the issue of immigration, the People's Party's 13 percent of the vote helped deprive the Social Democrats of the largest number of seats in parliament for the first time since the party's formation in 1924. A majority of blue-collar workers backed the People's Party and the Liberal Party.

In France, the issue of immigration had become interwoven with the issue of Islamic integration as early as the 1980s when a controversy broke out over Muslim girls wearing head scarves to school. In 1995, an Islamic group set off bombs in the Paris subway. In April 2002, French concern over Islamic immigration, reinforced by the September 11 attacks, played a role in Jean-Marie Le Pen's second place finish over Jospin, who had legalized 80,000 immigrants who had entered France illegally.

The same concerns also contributed to an astonishing election in the Netherlands. In the Netherlands, the major party leadership strongly supported immigration and the ideal of a multicultural Holland. When Hans Janmaat, the leader of the dissident Center Democrats, declared in 1997 that "Holland is not a country of immigrants" and "we will abolish the multicultural society as soon as we get the chance and power," he was indicted and convicted for inciting racial hatred. In 2002, in the wake of September 11, Pim Fortuyn, a colorful public speaker and magazine columnist who had been kicked out of another party because of his anti-Islamic views, established his own party, the Pim Fortuyn List, and campaigned against Islam's influence in Holland. Fortuyn was assassinated nine days before the election by a leftwing activist who objected to his attacks on Islam, but in the election, Fortuyn's party still took 17 percent of the vote, making it the second largest in parliament. Without Fortuyn, the party eventually fell apart, but it was succeeded in 2006 by Geert Wilders's highly successful Party for Freedom.

Populists and the Welfare State

As populist parties gained support for their stand against immigration, they widened their political base. The first populist parties, such as the National Front and the Freedom Party, had been petit-bourgeoisie parties. Their members were drawn primarily from small towns in the countryside, and were small business proprietors and small farmers—many of the same groups that had launched populism in the United States and spearheaded the rightwing in Europe between the world wars. But in the 1990s, Europe's populist parties grew largely by expanding their base into working-class constituencies that had formerly supported Social Democrats, Socialists, Laborites, and Communists. In France, Le Pen's National Front began winning support in blue-collar towns in the north. Voters who had backed Socialist François Mitterrand in the 1988 presidential race accounted for one-third of Le Pen's support in the 1995 presidential contest. "We are the party of the working class," Le Pen boasted.

That wasn't just because these parties were critical of immigrants. It was also because these parties, which had once reflected the anti-tax, anti-government views of small business began to embrace parts of the social democratic agenda on welfare and government. In France, Le Pen's National Front became a defender of the welfare state. It no longer called for the abolition of the income tax. Denmark's People's Party broke with its parent group's anti-tax focus. It became a defender of Denmark's generous public sector, with the proviso that its benefits be limited to Danes. Norway's Progress Party took a similar tack in the 1997 elections.

In Austria in the early 1990s, the Freedom Party, which had been steadfastly libertarian in its economics, took advantage

104 of the dominant parties' embrace of neoliberalism. In order to prepare for EU membership, the Social Democratic Party and Austrian People's Party, working in a "grand coalition," had championed massive privatization of Austria's industries, which led to the loss of about 100,000 jobs. In response to the public clamor over the move, the Freedom Party became a defender of the welfare state and critic of the EU's economics and globalization. The strategy worked. In the 1986 elections, 10 percent of the party's voters were blue-collar workers; by 1999, 47 percent were. Rightwing populist parties got the same kind of results throughout Western Europe. Thanks to the reaction to immigration and neoliberalism, what had been petit-bourgeois parties had become workers' parties.

The Founding of the European Union

The final reason for the rise of the populist right was the operation of the European Union and of the Eurozone. After World War II, French and German leaders, eager to avoid another continental war, took the first steps in integrating their economies. In 1951, France and West Germany, along with the Netherlands, Luxembourg, Belgium, and Italy, established the European Coal and Steel Community on lands that the two world wars had been fought over. In 1957, the six nations established a free trade area, the European Economic Community. Then in 1992 at Maastricht, the six, plus Greece, Spain, Portugal, the UK, Ireland, and Denmark, took the fateful step of setting up a European Union, within which goods and people could move freely. The countries, except for Denmark and the UK, also committed themselves to a common currency, the Euro, which would begin circulating in 1999.

France and Germany were always the main movers behind the EU; their principal motive was to integrate Germany into a

European community. But economics also figured in the design of the EU. Once, after the United States abandoned Bretton Woods, Europe's currencies began floating in value, and smaller countries like the Netherlands that were dependent on exports wanted to provide some stability to their currencies. Former French Finance Minister Dominique Strauss-Kahn described the Euro as "a tool to help us . . . resist irrational shifts in the market." The French also thought (mistakenly) that by subordinating the Deutsche-mark to a European Central Bank, which would be in charge of the Euro, France would no longer be subordinate to Germany's economy. And lesser economies like those of Spain, Greece, or Italy wanted the lower interest rates and greater foreign investment that they expected would come from having the same currency as the Germans and French. But whether wittingly or not, the EU and Eurozone institutionalized the rule of neoliberalism.

To accept the subordination of their currency to the Euro, the Germans demanded and got agreement from the other countries to a Stability and Growth Pact that put the ECB in charge of limiting members' deficits to 3 percent of GDP and debt to 60 percent of GDP. The Eurozone members believed that by limiting deficits, they would limit domestic inflation and therefore would keep the relationship among their countries in balance. This proved to be mistaken, but together with the creation of the Euro itself, the Stability and Growth Pact did have the effect of ruling out Keynesian strategies for economic recovery. The Keynesian strategy had relied on running deficits. If the deficits threatened to upset the trade balance, the country could use tariffs or a devaluation to protect its balance of payments. But devaluations were now impossible and tariffs forbidden. As a result, the dominant center-left or center-right parties found themselves hamstrung in the face of economic downturns and open to challenge from the populist right and left.

106   In its founding, the EU also adopted a principle of freedom of movement for people and businesses ("freedom of establishment") among its member nations. That reflected a desire to establish a common identity among the nations that had been at war with each other. But it also reflected business priorities. As the EU expanded eastward, European businesses in the West liked the idea of being able to import lower-wage labor from the East for restaurants, hotels, and construction without having to file papers. And businesses in the higher-wage West were now free to move their factories to the lower-wage East, as many began to do.

Labor unions grumbled at the freedom of establishment, while the rightwing populists took aim at the policy of open borders, which had the effect of undermining member countries' efforts to control immigration and asylum-seeking. Open borders meant, for instance, that legal or illegal immigrants or asylum seekers from North Africa could migrate from France or Italy to the Netherlands or Denmark. During the debate in Denmark in 1998 over the ratification of the Treaty of Amsterdam, which affirmed the EU's acceptance of open borders, the "no" vote ran a campaign headlined, "Welcome to 40 million Poles."

But the EU's administration was insulated from these protests. The EU's economic and immigration policies were chosen and reviewed by the member countries, but in such a way that the average citizen had little input into them. Of the EU's principal institutions, only one, the European Parliament, was elected directly—and it only had the power to approve or disapprove proposals and budgets submitted by the European Commission, whose members were appointed by the leaderships of the member states. The European Commission oversaw the daily operations of the EU, including its bureaucracy. The European Central Bank was controlled by a council of representatives from member banks. The European Court of Justice was appointed by member states. It was to issue rulings, but its deliberation and opinions were kept secret. In his prescient book about the European Union, Perry Anderson wrote, "What the core structures of the EU effectively do is to convert the open agenda of parliaments into the closed world of chancelleries."

Some leaders of the populist right were initially in favor of the EU. Jean-Marie Le Pen saw it as a vehicle for French dominance of the continent and a bulwark against Soviet communism. In the National Front's 1985 platform, he wrote, "The European Union will remain utopia as long as the Community doesn't have sufficient resources, a common currency and a political will, which is inseparable from the ability to defend itself." But after the fall of the Soviet Union and after it had become clear that that the EU would have a will of its own, Le Pen soured on it, comparing Maastricht to the Treaty of Troyes, which in the fifteenth century ceded the throne of France to England.

Other populist parties joined in rejecting the EU's "democracy deficit." The Danish People's Party called for Denmark to leave the EU. The Swedish Democrats declared, "European cooperation is a good thing, but a new European superstate is not." The populist parties' unhappiness with the EU was shared by many European voters. In preparation for signing the treaty at Maastricht, France and Denmark held referenda. The French barely approved the treaty by 51.1 percent, and the Danes defeated it by a similar margin, narrowly approving it later after Denmark was allowed to opt-out of several provisions. After the EU invited Norway to join, 52.2 of its voters turned membership down. Sweden's voters narrowly approved membership by 52.8 percent. In September 2000, 53.2 percent of Danes voted against joining the Eurozone; and three years later, 56.1 percent

108   of Swedes rejected the Eurozone.

In response to widespread dissatisfaction with the EU's structure, the federation's leadership adopted a new constitution that made minor adjustments. But in 2005, 54.9 percent of French voters and 61.5 percent of Dutch voters rejected the constitution. At that point, the EU withdrew the constitution, and relabeled it a treaty so that it would not have to be subject to popular ratification. That sparked cries of bureaucratic manipulation. Within the EU, opposition to the new constitution was led by the populist right parties, and as with their opposition to immigration, Islam, and neoliberal austerity, it boosted their support among the public. It also allowed those parties, which had been tainted by their links to European authoritarianism, to claim the mantle of democracy.

The Limits of Leftwing Populism: Syriza and Podemos

From 2003 through 2007, Europe seemed to be in passable shape. Growth in Europe averaged a low, but not disastrous 2.75 percent a year. The unemployment rate fell from 9.2 percent to 7.2 percent. The populist wave receded. But the financial crash that spread to Europe in late 2008 and the growth in refugees and Islamist terrorism that seemed to be tied to Western interventions and civil wars in the Middle East, South Asia, and North Africa sparked a populist revolt.

This populist reaction was different from the 1990s in one important respect. In the northern tier, where the Great Recession did not strike as forcefully, and where many of the asylum-seekers clustered, rightwing populism predominated. But in Southern Europe, where unemployment reached Great Depression levels, a new leftwing populism emerged in Spain, Greece, and Italy. When the major center-left and center-right parties, hobbled by their country's membership in the Eurozone, failed to revive their nation's economies, voters began looking to the new populist parties in these countries for answers.

110   The Eurocrisis

The financial crash, which surfaced in the United States in September 2008 with the collapse of Lehman Brothers, spread by the year's end to European banks, which had heavily invested in American derivatives. Credit dried up, borrowers defaulted, investment lagged, and unemployment rose. By 2009, the EU's average unemployment rate was 9.6 percent; in 2012, it would be 11.4 percent. And it would be far worse in Southern Europe—18 percent in Spain in 2009 and 25.1 percent in 2012. By 2012, the United States would begin pulling out of the Great Recession, but in Southern Europe it would endure, and would call into question the viability of the EU and the Euro.

In the United States, the immediate cause of the crash was financial deregulation and fraud. In Western Europe, the cause of the deepening recession was perverse financial regulation. The Eurozone, which went into effect in 1999, included 19 nations at varying degrees of economic development and with very different kinds of economies. Germany and the Netherlands, for instance, were export-driven high-tech economies. Under Gerhard Schröeder, German unions had agreed to restrain their wage demands. As a result, German wages actually ran behind productivity in the 2000s, making German products extremely competitive within the EU and internationally, and resulting in soaring trade surpluses.

Spain and Greece, by contrast, had lower-tech economies that relied on construction, tourism, financial services, and agriculture. Until they joined the Eurozone, these economies had managed to keep their current accounts balanced at moments of crisis by devaluing their currency. (Spain had devalued its currency four times between 1992 and 1995.) But when they joined the Eurozone, they no longer had control of their exchange rates.

What they lost in flexibility, however, they seemed initially to gain in attractiveness for foreign investors. In the past, foreign investors might have worried that they would lose money if one of these countries got in trouble and devalued its currency. But with the Euro, regulated by the ECB, that wouldn't happen in Spain any more than it would happen in Germany.

So in the early 2000s, when Spain and Greece (as well as the other PIIGS, Portugal, Ireland, and Italy) ran large trade deficits, foreign investors, led by Germany, plowed their trade surpluses back into these deficit countries in the form of bank loans and bond purchases. In the 2000s, the demand-driven and economies enjoyed a boom in office, home, and hotel construction; they were able to sell their government bonds; salaries and wages rose above productivity; and unemployment fell. Their membership in the Eurozone seemed to be an unmitigated blessing.

But when the financial crash hit, credit dried up internationally, home and office buyers began defaulting, investors began pulling out of these countries. The Spanish and Greek banks that had funded the new hotels and housing developments and office buildings were suddenly stuck with billions in bad loans. (Even today, the area outside Madrid is dotted with large unfinished housing developments.) With the banks threatening to go under, the Spanish and Greek governments attempted to bail them out, but that merely transferred the bad loans and the debts from private banks into the public sector, and created a "sovereign debt crisis."

These debts proved a mortal risk to these countries. As the debts mounted, the bond rating agencies lowered the countries' ratings, and interest rates on their payments rose, enlarging, in effect, the debts themselves. To repeat: under normal circumstances, these countries could have begun to dig themselves out of a fiscal hole through a devaluation, but that option was closed as long as they remained in the Eurozone. That left three options. First, they could convince the creditor countries, chiefly but not exclusively Germany, to forgive their debts. That proved impossible. The German electorate, along with the Finns and Dutch, loudly protested any bailout. Second, they could leave the Eurozone entirely and accept radical devaluation of their new currency. But voters in these countries didn't want to leave the Eurozone. They feared chaos and, particularly among the elderly, the loss of savings and of fixed incomes. Or third, these countries could undertake a severe version of what Mitterrand had to do in 1982—curtail spending and raise taxes resulting in even higher unemployment, but also a reduced demand for imports, and eventually and hopefully, by lowering wage costs, more competitive exports.

Greece was one of the first countries unable to service its debts. When the center-right New Democracy Party, which controlled the government, asked for aid from the "Troika" of the European Commission, ECB, and IMF, the Troika demanded in exchange that Greece take harsh austerity measures to shrink the public sector, reduce wages, raise taxes, and privatize public assets. Facing protests, the New Democracy government balked and called new elections, which the Panhellenic Socialist Movement (PASOK) under George Papandreou won.

When economist Yanis Varoufakis, who was then advising PASOK, advocated defaulting on the debts, the leadership dismissed such an idea as "treasonous." Seemingly at a loss, the Socialist government signed a memorandum in May 2010 with the Troika that in exchange for 110 billion Euros in loans, which would be recycled back to the original creditors, Greece would undertake harsh austerity measures. These included massive

budget cuts and a sharp increase in Greece's value added tax
(VAT). These measures depressed demand and led to higher
unemployment. Due to the closure of businesses, they also
increased the budget deficit. "The sovereignty of Greece will be
massively limited," Jean-Claude Juncker, the former president of
the European Commission, boasted.

After settling with Greece, the Troika dealt with Spain,
which was also being ruled in 2010 by socialists, the Spanish
Socialist Workers' Party, or PSOE. In exchange for 50 billion
Euros in loans, the Spanish government agreed to sharp budget
cuts, including the end to a family allowance provision and the
reduction of old-age insurance through extending the retire-
ment age. After the Socialist government had been voted out of
office in November 2011 and replaced by the center-right People's Party, the Spanish government agreed to even more draconian budget cuts, including a big increase in the VAT, and a
labor law that would make it much easier for employers to fire
workers.

Measures of austerity like this can work, as Thatcher's
experience in the 1980s showed, but only when the country
undergoing them already has viable export industries (which
can include financial services) *and* is surrounded by countries
with buoyant economies that are eager to buy imported goods
and services and to invest in lower-wage industries. Greece did
not benefit from either of these conditions—and Spain only
benefited marginally. In Greece, the Troika's austerity measures
merely made things even worse, and led to further bailout talks,
and to additional measures of austerity. These measures also
sparked a populist revolt directed against the EU's false promises of prosperity and against both the Socialist and center-right
parties that had agreed to them.

Syriza's Ascent to Power

Greece only emerged from the shadow of dictatorship in 1974 when the ruling colonels were forced out by their own military sponsors after they provoked a war with Turkey in Cyprus. Constantine Karamanlis and New Democracy won elections the next year, but in 1981, the Socialists under Andreas Papandreou, the father of George, took office, and with occasional interruptions from New Democracy, remained in power for most of the next thirty years.

PASOK succeeded in creating a low-grade version of social democracy in Greece, with a system of pensions, a National Health Service, and a public sector at roughly the size—16 percent of GDP—of some other EU states. What PASOK failed to do was limit the high degree of tax evasion from the country's wealthy and from its large shadow economy, or reform the parties' practice of using the state sector as a bribe-taking patronage machine. Tax evasion deepened the nation's deficits, and corruption by public officials bred distrust of both major parties, opening the way to a challenge to their rule from the left.

Greece's Communist Party had emerged from the dictatorship divided between an exterior wing that had remained out of the country and was totally subordinate to the Soviet Union and an interior "Eurocommunist" wing that sought to make Greece a democratic member of the European community. In 1989, with the Cold War waning, the two wings of the party came together to form Synaspismos, the Coalition of the Left and Progress. The remains of the pro-Soviet Communist Party eventually split off, but in 2004, what remained of Synaspismos joined with feminist and environmental groups to form Syriza, which stood for "coalition of the radical left." Syriza was initially a loose coalition that ran joint candidates, and its first efforts were decidedly mediocre. In the 2004 elections, it got only 3 percent of the vote, and even as late as October 2009, when the onset of the financial crash would sweep the Socialists back in power with 43.9 percent of the vote, Syriza only got 4.6 percent.

But the subservient response of the Socialists and the New Democrats to the EU's demand for austerity transformed Greek politics. Starting in May 2010, when the Socialist government agreed to the EU's demand for steep budget cuts, hundreds of thousands of demonstrators took to the streets in Athens and elsewhere. Many of the demonstrators were students and unemployed youth, but they were joined by striking workers. At the June 2012 elections, Syriza, headed by Alexis Tsipras, a civil engineer who had been a member of the communist youth organization and later the secretary of Synaspimos's youth organization, ran a campaign targeted at the Socialists' concessions to the EU. Syriza promised to rescind the memorandum with the EU, nationalize Greece's banks, raise taxes on the wealthy, and suspend debt repayment until Greece had recovered from the recession. This time, Syriza came in second to New Democracy with an astounding 26.9 percent of the vote. PASOK, discredited by its embrace of austerity, came in a distant third with only 12.3 percent. It has still not recovered from this vote.

In the 2012 elections, Syriza did best among young voters, the unemployed, and the urban employed in both public and private sectors. It did worst among housewives, senior citizens, and rural voters. While the party had its roots in the Eurocommunist left, Syriza shifted in 2012 to making a populist appeal. In 2009, Tsipras had barely referred to the "people," but in 2012, it became the constant referent in his speeches—occurring 51 times in his closing electoral address in June. In his speech,

116   Tsipras declared about the coming vote, "Sunday is not just about a simple confrontation between Syriza and the political establishment of the Memorandum. . . . It is about an encounter of the people with their lives. An encounter of the people with their fate. . . . Between the Greece of the oligarchy and the Greece of Democracy."

After its success in the 2012 elections, Syriza ceased to be a coalition and became a united party under Tsipras's leadership. As it prepared for the January 2015 elections, it again focused its platform on rejecting agreements with the Troika—and this now included New Democracy's even more onerous agreement of 2012. "We will prevent our country from being turned into a debt colony," its platform declared. Varoufakis, who had left PASOK and would later become Syriza's finance minister, accused New Democracy's government of "acting like a model prisoner, obeying the Troika's instructions, while, on the side, pleading for a rationalization of the imposed policies, terms, and conditions." Some Syriza members wanted to abandon the Euro altogether, but the party's official position was that it wanted to remain in the Eurozone, but not under the conditions that the Troika had imposed. That set up a populist confrontation with New Democracy and with the Troika.

In the January elections, Greece's voters affirmed Syriza's stand and repudiated the New Democracy government. Syriza carried the legislature and the election with 36.3 percent of the vote to New Democracy's 27.8 percent. (PASOK got a mere 4.7 percent.) Under Greek election law, the winner gets extra votes, so by gaining the support of the small Independent Greeks Party, Syriza took over the government. In February 2015, Tsipras and Varoufakis began negotiating with the Troika for a loan that would allow them to fend off the ECB and IMF, to whom Greece owed payments.

Both men came out fighting, Tsipras announcing that "the Troika is over." But as the negotiations proceeded, the IMF, the ECB, and the EU ministers, led by Germany, which had become the dominant power in the EU and its administration, held tough, demanding still more cuts in spending and tax increases as a condition for new loans, and rejecting the Greeks' plea to forgive part of their debt. Finally, in July, having defaulted on the loan payment to the IMF, Tsipras called for a referendum on whether to accept the Troika's deal. At Syriza's urging, 62 percent of Greeks voted to reject the Troika's offer. The stage seemed set for a final showdown between the Greek people and the Troika.

But Tsipras astonished Greek voters and many in his own party by returning to the talks and agreeing to terms that were even more onerous than the Troika had demanded earlier. More spending cuts, more tax increases, the evisceration of Greece's old-age pensions, new taxes on small and medium businesses that had been the heart blood of Greece's economy, and the sale of the state's remaining assets. Economist Paul Krugman termed the deal "madness." Wrote Krugman, "The European project—a project I have always praised and supported—has just been dealt a terrible, perhaps fatal blow. And whatever you think of Syriza, or Greece, it wasn't the Greeks who did it."

Unemployment in Greece remained at 25 percent and youth unemployment at double that. And Europe's economy remained stagnant. Economists Heiner Flassbeck and Costas Lapavitsas wrote, "The picture that emerges for Greece in view of these trends is simply appalling. The country appears trapped in low-growth equilibrium with exceptionally high unemployment and without command over the instruments of economic policy that could alter its predicament. The notion that low wages coupled with deregulation of markets and privatization of public assets

118 would lead to sustained growth is entirely without theoretical and empirical foundation."

In the wake of the agreement, Tsipras called for new elections in September as a vote of confidence. With turnout down, Syriza edged the New Democracy again by 35.5 to 28.1 percent, but as Tsipras and Syriza near their second year of rule, their prospects have darkened. The Troika—now joined by a new institution, the European Stability Mechanism, making it a Quartet—continues to be in charge of Greek economic policy, and continues to force further austerity in exchange for bridge loans. Tsipras's government complained about the terms but then, with a narrow 153—147 edge in the Greek parliament, acceded to the Quartet's demand. In January and again in May, huge protests greeted the new austerity measures, including a three-day general strike. In polls in May 2015, Syriza trailed New Democracy.

PASOK has virtually disappeared, but in an odd way, Syriza has replaced it as the center-left component of Greece's two-party monopoly. Syriza no longer fights the establishment, but has in effect become the center-left component of it, as PASOK was. It no longer advances demands that separate the people from an intransigent elite, but instead tries to nip away at the margins of the bad deal forced upon it by the Troika-turned-Quartet. Economist James Galbraith, who advised Syriza, thinks it still has "a radical constituency that . . . would rally to any authentic opposition force if one existed—which has proved for various reasons objectively impossible." He acknowledges that it now "operates as the unwilling agents of the Berlin finance ministry."

Political theorist Stathis Kouvelakis, who served on Syriza's central committee, but quit over the July deal with the Troika, says that the only way to put Greece back together is for it to leave the Eurozone. "It's impossible to fight austerity or neoliberalism within the framework of the existing monetary union, and, most

likely, of the EU as such. A rupture is indispensable," he says. But
if such a rupture was ever possible in the days after the July referendum, the moment for it seems to have passed. As a populist party promising to fight against the forces trying to impose austerity upon the country, Syriza appears to have failed. And that has had repercussions for other leftwing populist groups on the continent, particularly Podemos in Spain.

Podemos: Yes We Can

Spain, like Greece, never experienced the post-World War II flowering of social democracy that many of the countries in northern Europe did. Until December 1975, Spain was ruled by dictator Francisco Franco. After Franco's death, his appointed heir King Juan Carlos de Borbon and Adolfo Suárez, one of Franco's top lieutenants, arranged for a parliamentary transition. They wanted to be part of Europe. Spanish philosopher Ortega y Gasset had written earlier, "Spain is the problem, and Europe is the solution." Suárez's Union of the Democratic Centre (UCD) won the first election in 1977 and the newly legalized Spanish Socialist Workers' Party (PSOE) came in second. Spain joined NATO in 1982—an important step in taming the Spanish military. But with a recession paralyzing Spain's economy, the UCD decisively lost the election that year to Felipe Gonzalez and the PSOE, which would rule Spain for the next fourteen years.

The PSOE (pronounced peh-soy) is Spain's oldest existing party, founded in 1879. It emerged from the Franco years as a Marxist, revolutionary party, but Gonzalez convinced its membership to remove any hint of Marxism from the party's platform and to fashion itself as a multi-class rather than simply a working-class party. In the 1982 campaign, Gonzalez still advocated nationalizing Spain's banks, creating almost a million new jobs through government spending, and leaving NATO, but he reneged on all these promises. Faced with 16.5 percent unemployment *and* 14.4 percent inflation, influenced by what had happened to Mitterrand in France, and eager to join the European Economic Community, Gonzalez adopted a Thatcherite strategy of reducing inflation through tight money and high interest rates. While the unemployment rate soon exceeded 20 percent, inflation began to go down.

Gonzalez initially won the grudging support of the labor movement for his economic strategy, but by 1986, Spain's unions were up in arms, and staged two general strikes that frightened Gonzalez. Gonzalez then increased government spending, laying the basis for a rudimentary welfare state. But a steep recession began in 1992. That, combined with growing charges of corruption—endemic to Spain's patronage-based party system—contributed to PSOE losing the 1996 election to the People's Party (PP), a right-center party that had replaced the UCD as the principal opposition. Over the next two decades, the PP and PSOE have exchanged rule in the same way as Greece's PASOK and New Democracy once did.

In 2004, after eight years of PP rule, Spain elected PSOE's José Luis Rodriguez Zapatero. Zapatero widened the scope of welfare payments and increased the minimum wage, but faced with the global financial crisis, and pressure from ECB, Zapatero signed a memorandum in 2010 to raise taxes and cut spending, and on May 12 that year, announced large spending cuts. Zapatero was following the same path as Papandreou in Greece. A year later on May 15, young demonstrators gathered at Madrid's Puerta del Sol, where they began a month-long sit-in that spread throughout Spain.

The occupiers, dubbed the "Indignados" (outraged), were protesting Zapatero's spending cuts, bank evictions of people unable to pay their mortgages, unemployment, and continuing

corruption in the two major parties. (One sign read, "Democracy
is a two-party dictatorship.") The leaders weren't affiliated with
any political party, and spurned identification with the organized left and the labor movement. "We are neither right, nor
left, we are coming from the bottom and going for the top," a
slogan proclaimed. The protests spread to 57 other cities, and
at one point involved as many as 100,000 protesters in Madrid.
The demonstrators held assemblies and made proposals. Afterward, many of them continued to meet and demonstrate. In the
November 2011 general election, PSOE suffered its worst defeat
ever at the hands of the PP, and Mariano Rajoy became prime
minister.

Pablo Iglesias, a young leftwing political scientist at Complutense University in Madrid, had begun a television debate
show similar to William F. Buckley's *Firing Line*. The show
became remarkably popular and the ponytailed Iglesias became
a household name. In 2013, as unemployment rose to 26.3 percent in the wake of new spending cuts that Rajoy had imposed
at the ECB's behest, Iglesias and other Complutense colleagues
began discussing a political party that would capture the energy
of the Indignados.

Iglesias had been a member of the youth wing of Spain's
Communist Party, which after failing to build an electoral following in post-Franco Spain, had founded a coalition party
called the United Left in 1986 that included peace groups and
feminist groups. But Iglesias had drifted away from the Communists' hardline Marxism. When he approached them about
joining forces, they dismissed him as having "the principles of
Groucho Marx." In January 2014, Iglesias and other colleagues
from Complutense University announced the formation of a
new party, Podemos (We Can)—whose name echoed Obama's
presidential campaign slogan.

The party's leadership consisted of political scientists and the leaders from some of the groupuscules that had been part of the May 15 movement. Most were in their thirties or younger. (Several leaders that I interviewed looked as if they would have been carded if they had tried to order a drink at a bar in the United States.) The new party wouldn't be organized like a conventional party. It would make ample use of television and social media to draw people together and to get its message across. It would also have a different political outlook from conventional leftwing groups.

Iglesias and his two closest associates, fellow political scientists Juan Carlos Monedero and Íñigo Errejón, were enthusiastic supporters of the "pink tide" that was sweeping Latin America. It had begun with Hugo Chavez's election in Venezuela in 1999 and continued with Evo Morales's victory in Bolivia in 2006. Chavez and Morales had rejected the classic socialist strategy of championing the working class against the capitalist class and had instead embraced a populist strategy of rallying their country's "bravo pueblo" against the oligarchs. Iglesias and Monedero had become advisors to Chavez, and Errejón had written his doctoral thesis at Complutense on Morales's revolution. (It would later come out that Monedero had been paid handsomely by Chavez.)

Monedero, who at 51 was the old man of the party and who had been the director of the United Left, was a more orthodox leftist, but Iglesias and Errejón combined the example of Latin American populism with the work of "post-Marxist" political philosophers like Ernesto Laclau, an Argentinian who taught at Essex University, and his wife, Belgian Chantal Mouffe. "A recent political initiative in our country would not have been possible," Errejón later declared, "without the intellectual confirmation and learning from the processes of change in Latin

America" and without "an understanding of the role of speech, common sentiment, and hegemony that is clearly indebted to the work of Laclau."

Laclau and Mouffe contended that the old leftwing categories of "working class" and "socialism" were obsolete and had to be replaced with a populist project pitting the people against elites and aimed at creating "radical democracy." The goal of a populist party was to knit diverse groups into a "people" united by a set of demands that created an ideological "frontier" between the people and the elite. Unlike other European intellectuals, Laclau and Mouffe defined populism as a logic that could take either left or rightwing form. Errejón became an eager disciple—in 2015, he published a book of conversations between him and Mouffe that became a bible for Podemos cadres—and Iglesias in the first years of Podemos also endorsed Laclau and Mouffe's view of populism.

Iglesias and Errejón called for a conflict between "la gente" and "la casta,"—the latter a Spanish word, but a concept borrowed from the Italian and used by Beppe Grillo. The term referred to the major political and economic interests in Spain, or as Iglesias put it more colloquially in his book, *Politics in a Time of Crisis*, "the thieves who erect political frameworks for stealing democracy from the people." Iglesias and Errejón defined the conflict as being between the people and the elites rather than between "left" and "right." Influenced, perhaps, by the attitude of the Indignados, they saw Spain's left as stagnant and irrelevant— the United Left hadn't mounted a significant electoral challenge in almost two decades. The new party, Errejón explained in *Le Monde Diplomatique*, "would start a process or at least make possible a new political frontier which symbolically postulates the existence of a people not represented by the dominant political castes, and which is beyond left and right metaphors."

They also worried that the major parties would marginalize them by defining them as "the left." Iglesias warned that "when our adversaries dub us the 'radical left' and try, incessantly to identify us with its symbols, they push us onto a terrain where their victory is easier." In his dialogue with Mouffe, Errejón explained that "the elite were very comfortable with the left-right axis. They located themselves at the center-right/center-left, and placed the 'challengers'—those who defied them—at the margins."

Iglesias and Errejón were personally of the left (Podemos's bookstore in its Madrid café is filled with back copies of *New Left Review* and works by contemporary Marxists like David Harvey), but following Laclau and Mouffe, they didn't define Podemos's objective as socialism. "We openly acknowledge we are not opposing a strategy for a transition to socialism," Iglesias told *New Left Review*, "but we are being more modest and adopting a neo-Keynesian approach, like the European left, calling for higher investment, security, social rights, and redistribution." When I asked Segundo González Garcia, a top Podemos leader and a member of Parliament, whether they took any of the Latin American countries as models, he said, "We want our country to be closer to Northern Europe. Our model is closer to Sweden and Norway than Latin America. We want a welfare state, a guaranteed income." (Spain's welfare state, even before the spending cuts, was far less robust than those of the EU's northern tier.)

Podemos, like Syriza, was an anti-austerity party contesting the EU's rules and the Spanish government's capitulation to them. Iglesias described Podemos's goal as "post-neoliberalism." Its program that first year called for ending evictions, creating a government-funded guaranteed annual income, auditing Spain's debt with a view to not paying what was "illegitimate," making the Stability and Growth Pact "flexible" and making it

include "full employment" in its objectives, democratization of
Brussels and rejection of the Lisbon Treaty, repeal of Spain's
balanced budget law, and a 35-hour workweek. Together, these
demands established a divide between it and the government
and main political parties, as well as between the Spanish
people and Brussels.

By their own admission, Podemos's leaders thought that in
order to extricate Spain fully from the Eurocrisis, Spain would
eventually have to abandon the Euro itself, but they were aware
that Spain's voters, who had earlier prospered under the Euro,
were unwilling to contemplate breaking with the EU. After
decades of isolation under Franco, Spanish voters wouldn't
support a return to Spain's own currency. Nacho Álvarez, a col-
league of Iglesias at Complutense and Podemos's chief economist, told me, "No progressive force dares to speak about exiting
of the euro, basically because the southern populations do not
even want to hear about that and this is surely the only good
solution, or at least 'final' solution to recover democracy and
sovereignty." So they limited themselves to threatening to repudiate Spain's debt and demanding a reformulation of the Stability and Growth Pact.

As the European elections approached in May 2014, few
Spaniards had heard of Podemos. To publicize the party, the
leaders put the well known Iglesias's photo on their literature.
That, too, was consistent with a populist strategy of using a
leader as a unifying symbol. To their amazement, the party won
8 percent—a significant showing in a multi-party election—
and five seats. Podemos's success in the European elections
gave the party visibility, and as unemployment mounted, and
charges of corruption began flying against the PP government,
Podemos's poll numbers began to rise. From December 2014
through April 2015, polls for the forthcoming parliamentary

126 elections in December 2015 actually showed Podemos leading both PP and PSOE.

Podemos's hopes had initially been buoyed by Syriza's success in Greece. In Athens in January 2015, Iglesias joined Tsipras on stage for a closing campaign event. They danced together to a Leonard Cohen song, "First we take Manhattan, then we take Berlin," but changed the lyrics to "First we take Athens, then we take Madrid." But as the furious battle between Syriza and the Troika raged that winter, and as rumors circulated that Greece was going to exit the Eurozone, Iglesias, mindful of Spanish voters' commitment to Europe and the Euro, began backing away from Podemos's identification with Syriza. Iglesias removed a photograph of him and Tsipras from his Twitter feed. "Spain is not Greece," he now declared. Iglesias made clear that Podemos favored reforming, but not leaving the EU and the Eurozone. In addition, Podemos dropped its demand for an audit of the federal debt, which might have justified selective defaults, and for a universal living wage. But after the spectacle of the Greeks rejecting and then Syriza accepting the Troika's demands, Podemos plunged in the polls to as low as 10 percent, falling behind a new center-right anti-corruption party Ciudadanos, or Citizens.

The PP expected to win reelection. While unemployment was still 23.7 percent on the eve of the election, the economy had started growing, thanks in part to the ECB curiously ignoring a center-right government running deficits that exceeded the 3 percent limit. But Spain's political system was rife with bribes and kickbacks and as the election approached, 40 PP officials were scheduled to stand trial for a kickback scheme. In the end, the PP got 28.7 percent—the lowest percentage ever for a leading party—the PSOE 22 percent, and Podemos got an impressive 20.7 percent.

Podemos's voting base had some similarity to Sanders's voters, but was broader. Podemos won young voters and the voters in the large metropolitan areas. Both Madrid and Barcelona elected mayors affiliated with Podemos. By contrast, PP's base was middle and upper class, older and rural or small-town, while the PSOE retained its traditional working-class as well as its middle-class support. But once a two-party system, Spain has become a multi-party system. And as the results for the December election bore out, neither the PP and PSOE had won enough seats for a ready-made majority. The inconclusive result led to five months of wrangling among the parties, highlighted by PSOE's refusal to form a grand coalition with the PP and Podemos's refusal to subordinate itself to PSOE in a center-left coalition. The King finally called new elections for the end of June.

As the parties quarreled over the December results, a rift within Podemos opened up between Iglesias and Errejón. With new elections likely, Iglesias decided that Podemos needed to get enough votes and parliamentary seats to exceed PSOE. Podemos would then be able either to be the dominant party in a governing coalition of the left with PSOE, or if PSOE were to form a grand coalition with PP, become the leading opposition party. He cast his eye on the United Left, which had won 3.68 percent of the vote in December, and which together with Podemos's vote, would have put them over PSOE's total. In the face of Errejon's opposition to becoming a party of "the left," Iglesias decided to negotiate a coalition with the United Left, whose leadership had changed since 2013. He won their agreement to run a combined slate, Unidos Podemos, in the election.

Iglesias and Podemos acquired the promise of the United Left's votes without accepting its most radical measures, such as abolishing the monarchy and nationalizing banks. Eager to deflect any charges of extremism, Podemos crafted a platform for Unidos Podemos that was only a shade to the left of PSOE. Like PSOE, the groups promised that Spain would adhere to the Eurozone's stability pact, but asked for a "new path of deficit reduction" that would be "more gradual than that raised by the European Commission." They insisted (implausibly) that Spain could meet this deficit target through public investment rather than cuts in social spending; and they asked for a boost in social spending primarily on education and healthcare, while dropping the demand for a guaranteed annual income or 35-hour week. And instead of calling explicitly for the cancellation or reduction of national debts, they called for a European conference to propose "the restructuring of the debt in the Eurozone area."

In the polls leading up to the June 26 election, Unidos Podemos was running well ahead of PSOE and within striking distance of the PP. PSOE and PP struck back by highlighting Podemos's ties to Latin America's authoritarian populism (and the collapse of Venezuela's oil-based economy) and the communist presence in Unidos Podemos. (The headline in the pro-PSOE *El Pais* on the formation of Unidos Podemos read, "Podemos seals deal with communist group to run together in new election.") To counter these charges, Unidos Podemos further attempted to soften its image. In the last weeks, it published its program in the form of a 192-page IKEA catalogue with photos of people using housewares accompanied by a list of 394 largely anodyne "demands," which included an Animal Welfare Act, emotional intelligence, care for forests, and citizen participation in government.

In the election—held on June 26, three days after the British had voted to leave the European Union—Unidos Podemos landed in third with an embarrassing thud. The combined list of Podemos and the United Left got the same number of seats—71 of 350—that the two parties had gotten in December, but they actually received 1.09 million fewer votes, due largely to abstentions in areas that had been Podemos's strongholds in December. PP improved its showing, but still did not have enough seats to form a majority. PSOE got fewer votes than it had in December, but was still far ahead of Unidos Podemos. The bickering will go on, and there could even be another election, but Podemos will not play as significant a role in the bickering; if a majority is formed, Podemos will probably not hold the balance of power in a new parliament. Its attempt to displace PSOE as the major party of the left failed.

Monedero, who had left the party's formal leadership the year before after the story of his Venezuelan funding broke, but who still advised Iglesias, blamed Unidos Podemos's disappointing showing partly on the "campaign of fear" conducted by the PP and PSOE, but also on Unidos Podemos's failure to present a political alternative to the PSOE. Monedero charged that the campaign, which was run by Errejón, was "constantly filing down the rough edges" of its politics. It also relied, he charged, too much on conventional rallies and on television and eschewed militant street protests with students, social organizations, and unions. Monedero defended the alliance with the United Left, contending that Podemos would have done "even worse" without it. Errejon, in response, reiterated his opposition to having allied with the United Left. "Two plus two did not add up to four," he said. Errejon said that Podemos had been "trapped" by the alliance. "On the left-right axis, it is more difficult to build a new majority," he said. "On that axis, fields remain immobile."

Could Monedero and Errejon have both been right—and wrong? In the previous election, some voters had backed Podemos as a populist protest party against the PSOE and PP. But with polls suggesting that Unidos Podemos might actually win, they had evaluated it and Podemos as a governing party and found it wanting. As Errejón maintained, the alliance with the United Left had probably reinforced the "campaign of fear" So, too, did the British vote to leave the EU, which caused the Spanish stock market to plunge on the eve of the election, and may have led many voters to seek a safer and known harbor in the PSOE and PP.

Monedero also had a point. By watering down their demands, and failing to distinguish themselves from PSOE either in their demands or actions, Podemos had abandoned its populist stance for a center-left reformism and an appearance as just another political party. Their demands no longer established a frontier between the people and la casta. They were no longer clearly campaigning against la casta. That may have accounted for many of the abstentions in their political strongholds. Voters were no longer inspired by their message or the way it was delivered.

Syriza abandoned its populist stance when it had come up against the power of the Troika. It had become another left-center party with incremental ambitions. But by the time Syriza abandoned its populism, it had already displaced PASOK. Podemos has had no such luck. Spain's PSOE has lost support since Zapatero gave in to the Troika, but it remains one of Spain's two major parties, and in the June election, Podemos failed to displace it. So while Syriza, in the face of Greece's continuing slide, must decide how it can govern, Podemos must show it can recapture what propelled it to the brink of power in Spain.

Rightwing Populism on the March in Northern Europe

During the Eurocrisis, leftwing populist groups arose primarily in the south, while rightwing groups fared best in northern and central Europe. Much of this had to do with the rise in immigration there. In 2014, there were 280,000 migrants to Europe from the Middle East and North Africa; in 2015, the number grew to over a million. In 2000, 7.1 percent of Danes were first or second generation immigrants; in 2016, it was 12.3 percent. Sweden's immigrant population is 22.2 percent. In the United Kingdom, 630,000 immigrants arrived in 2015, which would have been equivalent to 3.2 million immigrants arriving in the U.S. that year.

The rise in immigration coincided with a rise in terrorist attacks, particularly in the north. From December 2010 to March 2016, there were nine major attacks in Europe. Four of the worst occurred in the last two years: In January 2015, the Charlie Hebdo massacre in Paris claimed 20; the November 2015 Paris attacks by ISIS killed 137; in Brussels in March 2016, three more ISIS suicide bombings left 35 dead; in July, a cargo truck drove into Bastille Day crowds in Nice, killing 85. In addition, there

132   were sexual assaults involving refugees and immigrants from the Middle East and North Africa—the best known occurring in Cologne on New Year's Eve 2015. Together, the flood of immigrants, the terrorist acts, and sexual assaults lent credence to two decades of agitation by rightwing populist groups against immigrants and Islam.

Denmark and Austria: Populism Amid Prosperity

Leftwing populist groups flourished in the least prosperous European economies. Rightwing populism has found a home in some of the more and most prosperous countries. These are the countries where immigrants and asylum-seekers have aspired to live. Denmark has one of the world's most successful economies. It has the second highest per capita income in the European Union, trailing only Luxembourg. In 2016 it had only 4.6 percent unemployment. It was virtually untouched by the Great Recession. Its Social Democratic government might have been expected to win reelection easily in the June 2015 election; and the Social Democrats did win 26.3 percent, the highest percentage of any party in the election, while the vote for their traditional opposition, the Liberals, fell 7 percentage points to 19.5 percent. But the Danish People's Party, campaigning on border controls, further restriction of immigration, and a critical approach to the EU, went from 12.3 in 2011 to 21.1 percent in the vote. They held the key to a ruling majority, and with their informal support the Liberals were able to displace the Social Democrats and form a government.

The People's Party didn't actually join the Liberal government, because they disagreed with the Liberal proposal to cut taxes for the rich. Explained Kenneth Kristensen Berth, who joined the party at its inception and is now a member of parliament and a party spokesman, "The problem was that the Liberal

Alliance said to the Prime Minister that he should deliver tax relief for the most wealthy in this country. We wouldn't go into government on the basis of tax relief for the most wealthy." Like other rightwing populists, the People's Party are strongly supportive of the welfare state, as long as spending is confined to Danish citizens. In fact on these issues, Berth acknowledged, they are closer to the Social Democrats. But they parted company with the Social Democrats and are aligned with the Liberals on preventing asylum seekers from establishing permanent residence in Denmark. "If we don't fix immigration, there is no reason to fix the rest," Berth says.

In exchange for informal support from the People's Party, the Liberals adopted the People's Party's agenda on immigrants, refugees, and Islam. They cuts benefits to refugees and immigrants by 45 percent; they required pork in school and day-care menus (to defy Islamic prohibitions on eating pork); they ordered the confiscation of refugees' cash and valuables that exceeded $1,450—a move eerily reminiscent of Nazi confiscation of Jewish valuables. These harsh stances reflected significant popular opinion.

According to one newspaper poll in January 2016, 70 percent of Danes thought refugees were the most important issue facing the country, and 37 percent opposed giving any more resident permits to refugees. Danish political experts, politicians, and journalists, including those opposed to the People's Party, told me they expected the People's Party to succeed politically. "I think they are going to get the government soon," said Rene Offersen, a prominent lawyer and Conservative Party member.

Austria, like Denmark, has enjoyed relative prosperity. Its unemployment rate from 2012 to 2016 hovered between 4.7 and 5.8 percent. But its citizens have also been up in arms over refugees. It had 90,000 requests for asylum in 2015, the

134   second most per capita in the EU. While there were no terrorist attacks on its soil, it had murders and rapes perpetrated
by recent migrants.

Since 2013, Austria had been ruled by a "grand coalition"
of the Social Democrats and the center-right People's Party,
with Social Democrat Werner Faymann serving as chancellor.
In 2015, Faymann joined German Chancellor Angela Merkel in
backing open borders for refugees, but when Faymann and his
party saw polls showing the rightwing populist Freedom Party
ahead in the forthcoming April presidential elections, Faymann
changed course. In March, he capped the number of refugees.
But it was too late.

In the April 2015 election, the Freedom Party candidate
Norbert Hofer got 34 percent of the vote, compared to 11 percent
each for the Social Democrat and People's Party candidates. In
a runoff in May, the Green Party candidate, Alexander Van der
Bellen, who had come in second in the first round, barely edged
out Hofer by 50.3 to 49.7 percent. But because of improper
counting of absentee ballots, Austrian courts ruled there will
have to be a revote in October 2016. The vote bore out the profile of many rightwing populist groups. Hofer captured nearly
90 percent of the vote among blue-collar workers and rural and
small town voters outside the main metropolises, while Green
Party candidate won white-collar voters and nine of ten cities.

UKIP: The Revolt of the Left-Behinds

Like Denmark and Austria, Great Britain, where the unemployment rate has been falling since September 2011 and is
now at 5.4 percent, has proven to be fertile ground for rightwing populism. Having led the successful fight to get Britain
to vote itself out of the EU, the United Kingdom Independence
Party (UKIP) has had the greatest impact on its country and

on the EU of any populist party. That vote reshuffled politics
and economics in the UK and has cast doubt on the long-term
future of the EU.

UKIP was founded in 1993, but remained a marginal
single-issue party and pressure group for almost two decades.
If it had an overall politics, it was anti-tax, economically libertarian, and socially conservative. Its primary base was in mid- to
upscale shires that generally voted Conservative. It got 1 percent
in the 1995 parliamentary elections, 2.2 percent in 2005 and 3.1
percent in 2010. Its success began to come in elections for the
European parliament where it got 16.1 percent in 2004 and 16.5
percent in 2009, second only to the Tories. That reflected the
rise in opposition to the EU.

Popular opposition to the EU went back decades and was
based on the perception that by joining the EU, the UK had
abandoned its own sovereignty. It drew on English or British
nationalism. But by 2009, opposition to the EU had begun to
spread from Tory towns to the working-class areas in Northern
and Eastern England that regularly voted for Labour. And UKIP
began to find voters there. According to Robert Ford and Matthew Goodwin's extensive study of UKIP and its supporters,
the bulk of its support shifted to the older less-educated and
primarily male white working class. This older working class
had turned against the EU and was backing the UKIP in some
elections.

Many of these new UKIP voters were clustered in smaller
towns that had once been centers of manufacturing and
mining, but that in the wake of Thatcher and the 1980s had
become industrial ghost towns. Their inhabitants were the
"left-behinds" of the UK's economic development. While
London, as a center of finance and financial and legal services,
and the universities, as incubators of high-tech development,

136   had prospered, Britain's older industrial areas had fallen into harder and harder times.

The growth in anti-EU sentiment among these voters was fueled by the rise of immigration to Britain from Eastern Europe. The biggest spike in immigration occurred after 2004. In that year, eight countries from Eastern Europe, including Poland, Hungary, and the Baltic states, joined the EU. In 2007, Romania and Bulgaria joined. According to EU rules, the UK could have instituted a seven-year transitional ban on emigration from these countries, but Tony Blair, who was then prime minister, didn't do so. By 2015, immigration had climbed to over 600,000 a year.

Londoners and residents of Great Britain's high-tech enclaves welcomed the new immigrants, but many working-class voters saw them as a further threat to their standard of living. During the Brexit campaign, there was an intense debate over whether, and if so how, immigrants had actually affected native-born workers, but there was some agreement, expressed by Theresa May, who was then Cameron's Home Secretary, and who favored remaining in the EU, that the recent flood of immigrants had put "pressure on public services, on housing, on infrastructure . . . it can hold down wages and push British workers out of jobs." Studies from the government's Migration Advisory Committee had concluded, for instance, that immigration "lowers wages at the bottom of the wage distribution" and that during slow growth or a downturn, "working-age migrants are associated with a reduction in native employment rates."

The growing opposition to immigration was cultural as well as economic, particularly among senior citizens who had grown up in a Britain when, as late as 1964, 98 percent of the electorate was white. According to a 2013 British Social Attitudes survey, among those over age 65, 69 percent thought immigration should be reduced "a lot," 66 percent would mind "if a close relative married a Muslim," 61 percent thought being born in Britain was "very important" to being British, and 58 percent tthought hat having British ancestors was "very important" to being British. By contrast, only 13 percent of those under 35 thought having British ancestors was very important to being British.

But as late as 2010, opposition to immigration hadn't translated into large-scale support for *leaving* the EU. That happened largely out of the efforts of UKIP leader Nigel Farage, who after the party's poor showing in the 2010 general election, set about honing UKIP's message of opposition to the EU. Farage fused the incendiary issue of immigration with that of EU membership. UKIP adopted the position that the way to limit immigration was to get out of the EU. Farage also adapted UKIP's general political outlook to its new working-class voters, many of whom had once voted for Labour. He abandoned UKIP's commitment to laissez-faire economics. Farage proposed taking the funds that the UK contributed to the EU and using them to improve Britain's National Health Service.

Farage framed UKIP's anti-immigrant and anti-EU sentiment in populist terms. UKIP claimed it was championing the people—the left-behinds—against London and Brussels's elites. Farage's success showed up in the 2014 European Union election, when UKIP came in first with 27.49 percent. That election was a clear indication that UKIP had put the issue of Britain's EU membership on the country's political agenda.

Within the Conservative Party, Prime Minister David Cameron had to contend with a group of back-benchers who also opposed Britain's membership in the EU, mainly British nationalists who represented the upscale areas where UKIP still had support. To appease them, Cameron had promised in 2013 that if he were reelected in the 2015 general election, he would hold

138   a referendum on EU membership. In the 2015 general election, Cameron was easily reelected against a lackluster Labour opponent. UKIP got a respectable 13 percent, with some of its votes coming at Labour's expense. After the election, Cameron set the referendum for June of 2016.

Cameron was confident that he could keep Britain within the EU. He and his Chancellor of the Exchequer George Osborne, joined by Britain's top business leaders and major newspapers, warned repeatedly that a decision to leave the EU could have dire economic consequences. Labour Party leader Jeremy Corbyn waged a halfhearted campaign for staying within the EU that probably failed to sway potential supporters among the "left-behinds" while further alienating what had once been Labour constituencies. UKIP led the campaign against the referendum along with two prominent Tories, former London Mayor Boris Johnson and former Cabinet member and MP Michael Gove.

Farage conducted the referendum campaign in classic populist fashion, pitting the people against the establishment. On May 20, he told reporters, "It is the establishment, it is the wealthy, it is the multi-nationals, it is the big banks, it is those whose lives have really done rather well in the last few years who are supporting remaining and against it is the people." Ten days later, he said, "This is our chance as a people to get back at a political class that has given away everything this nation has ever stood for, everything our forebears ever fought for and everything we want to hand on to our children and grandchildren." Farage was not above using incendiary imagery to promote his cause. One UKIP poster, called "Breaking Point," showed streams of dark-skinned Middle Easterners pouring into Slovenia, presumably en route to the UK.

In the referendum, UKIP and the dissident Tories were able to build a majority for leaving the EU out of the working-class left-behinds and the middle-class British nationalists. Within England, Remain won heavily in London and in the bigger cities, except for Birmingham and Sheffield, and in university towns. Leave won in blue-collar towns and in the middle-class areas where Euroskepticism had been strong. The working class was key. Voters for Leave were concentrated among older and less educated voters and within towns where the median income was less than $45,000.

The decision to leave was a major victory for UKIP and a major defeat for the two establishment parties and the political worldview they promoted—one in which professional and managerial classes prospered, but the older working class succumbed to the global forces of mobile labor and capital. Tony Blair told Sky News afterward, "The center-left and the center-right have lost their political traction. The populist insurgent movements on the left and right are taking control right now."

As Blair suggested, UKIP's rise, and the decision to leave the EU, were tied to rejection of the broader neoliberal worldview. In March 2015, journalist David Goodhart writing in the Labour magazine, *Prospect,* had made exactly this point in explaining UKIP's popularity:

> The modern social and economic liberalism, that dominates all the main political parties, has produced an economically abandoned bottom third of the population with no real chance of ever gaining a share in prosperity; and an even larger group who feel a vague sense of loss in today's atomized society in which the stability of family and the identity of place and nation has been eroded. UKIP voters are a compound of those ignored, abandoned, and laughed at by the metropolitan liberals who, despite some party differences, dominate our public and cultural life.

In the referendum, these voters had rejected not just the EU, but its underlying economic and social philosophy.

After the victory of Leave, UKIP leaders talked of displacing the Labour Party as Britain's second major party. Indeed, the referendum did show that there was a vacuum in British politics, particularly among what was once Labour's natural constituency. But the referendum's results didn't necessarily put UKIP into a position of filling it. Populist parties can suffer when their demands are peremptorily rejected, as Syriza's were by the Troika. Or they can suffer when their central demands are met, as with the People's Party in the United States.

Under Farage, UKIP had become more than a single-issue party, but the call to leave the EU was nevertheless the single demand that defined UKIP's defense of the people against the establishment. It was essential to its populist insurgency. Having won it, UKIP must now either redefine itself or slide into marginality. And it will have to do so, at least for the time, without Farage as its leader; after the referendum, Farage declared his own mission accomplished and resigned from his post at the head of the party.

Marine Le Pen and the National Front

Of all the EU's nations, France has been most directly affected by rising immigration and Islamist-inspired terrorist attacks. It also has Europe's most important rightwing populist party. In 2017, France will hold presidential and parliamentary elections. As of May 2016, the National Front's Marine Le Pen led in polls over the Republican and Socialist candidates. Were she to win the French presidency, it would upset the political balance across Europe. To do so, however, she will have to overcome the FN's reputation for rightwing extremism created by her father Jean-Marie Le Pen.

Jean-Marie Le Pen, the FN's founder, was a verbal bomb-
thrower who loved to *epater le bourgeois*—shock the bourgeoisie.
He reinforced the image of the FN as a defender of Vichy France
and as the voice of the French Pieds-Noirs who had angrily fled
Algeria during its war of independence. Le Pen also famously
declared the Holocaust a "detail" of World War II. And his top
lieutenants were cut from similar cloth. Bruno Gollnisch, who
was elected to the French National Assembly in 1986, was convicted in 2007 of Holocaust denial.

By reorienting the FN from opposing communists to
opposing immigrants and Islam, and by supplementing the
economic concerns of the shopkeeper with those of the unemployed steelworker, Le Pen added working-class voters in the
north to the FN's Catholic, provincial base in the south. That
led to Le Pen's astonishing second place showing in the 2002
runoff against the Socialist Prime Minister Lionel Jospin. But
Le Pen's success was short-lived. Fearful of a Le Pen victory,
Jospin and the Socialists advised their voters to support the
unpopular incumbent Jacques Chirac, the candidate of the
center-right Rally for the Republic, in the next round. As a
result, Chirac was able to rout Le Pen, 82 percent to 18 percent,
in the final runoff.

Le Pen's failure in the second round suggested that there
were strict limits to the FN's popularity. Too many voters identified the FN with the hated Vichy regime and thought of its
leader as an anti-Semitic extremist. As his daughter Marine Le
Pen put it, there was a "glass ceiling" that the FN could not break
through. The 2007 election appeared to confirm that. Nicolas
Sarkozy, who had been interior minister in Chirac's administration, and was running as the candidate of the center-right
UMP, took a hard line against the immigrant youths who had
rioted in 2005 and against immigrants in general. If they don't

142   "love France," he declared, they should "leave it," and he proposed cutting immigration. By coopting the FN position, Sarkozy doomed Le Pen, who came in fourth in the first round with only 10.44 percent.

In the first round of the legislative elections that year, the FN did even worse, getting only 4.29 percent and winning no seats. That imperiled the party's state campaign funding, which depended on its winning seats. In January 2011, Jean-Marie Le Pen, 82, decided to retire as the party chairman. That set up a leadership battle between Gollnisch and Marine Le Pen.

Marine Le Pen, who was born in 1968, was the youngest of Le Pen's three daughters. Her most vivid memory, recounted in her autobiography, *Against the Current*, was of someone blowing up their Paris home when she was eight in order to kill her father. No one was injured, but it was her introduction, she wrote, to a "world without pity." The next year, however, a wealthy patron without children left a fortune to Jean-Marie Le Pen, including a mansion in the Paris suburbs, where Marine and her sisters then grew up.

Marine Le Pen got a law degree and entered private practice, but in 1998, she took over the FN's legal department. She was elected a Regional Councilor from Nord-Pas-de-Calais, a beaten-down former mining region dominated by socialists and communists. Marine Le Pen is a tall, handsome bleached blonde with a commanding voice and quick wit. She has her father's toughness, and his willingness to withstand and then counter harsh criticism. She also shares her father's ardent French nationalism—she named her oldest daughter after Joan of Arc—as well as his opposition to immigrants who she believes challenge French values and culture. But she was of an entirely different political generation from her father and from many of the older FN followers.

Marine Le Pen is twice-divorced, pro-choice, and comfortable around gays. She did not inherit her father's anti-Semitism or his sympathy for Vichy or colonial France. In 2000, she became president of Generations Le Pen, a youth group whose mission in part was to alter the family's and the party's reputation. One of its groups was the National Circle of Jewish Frenchman.

In her autobiography, she blamed leftwing human rights groups such as SOS Racisme for demonizing the FN, but she admitted that the party had also contributed to its reputation by continuing to "create polemics" that "reinforced the caricature" of the organization. She didn't single out her father, but his views were exactly what she had in mind. In 2008, she broke publicly with him when, in an interview with a French magazine, he once again described the Nazi gas chambers as a "detail." "I do not share on these events the same vision," Marine Le Pen told the magazine. She was also critical of Gollnisch's comments on gas chambers.

In the 2011 election to head the FN, she defeated Gollnisch by two-to-one among the membership—as much because of her name as her views. But once installed as president and as the party's projected presidential candidate for 2012, she set about de-demonizing (*dédiabolisation*) the FN and turning it from a rightwing sect into a "party like the others." She changed the party's outlook in three key respects:

Anti-Semitism and pro-Vichy: Soon after becoming president of the FN, she condemned "what happened in the [concentration] camps as the height of barbarism" and made clear that anti-Semites and racists were not welcome in the party. She banned skinheads and anyone in combat-fatigues from the FN's first march. A FN circular said, "Marine Le Pen has warned that anything resembling a 'skinhead' in any shape or form will be

144   excluded by all necessary means." She also began citing favorably Charles de Gaulle—who was despised by her father and his generation of Vichy loyalists. She repeatedly rebuked her father for his anti-Semitic outbursts, finally expelling him from the party in August 2015.

Immigrants and Islam: Le Pen was no less vehement than her father in denouncing attacks by Islamists and in tying them to what she claimed were France's lax immigration policies. After a French Muslim of Algerian descent, who had been radicalized in Afghanistan, killed seven people in Toulouse in March 2012, Le Pen commented, "How many Mohammed Merahs arrive each day in France in boats or airplanes filled with immigrants? How many Mohammed Merahs are there among unassimilated children?" But Le Pen tried to create distinctions between what she was saying and past FN statements. She insisted she was not against Muslims or Muslim immigrants, but against those who violated French principles of *laïcité*—or secularism—by imposing their religion, either as politics or as cultural practices, on the public realm. "In France, we often say the U.S. is a multicultural society, but it's not. It's multiethnic, but one single culture. I don't say that nobody should enter our country. On the contrary, in the old days immigrants entered France and blended in. They adopted the French language and traditions. Whereas now entire communities set themselves up within France, governed by their own codes and traditions," she explained to an interviewer in 2011.

Economic Nationalism: Le Pen's biggest departure in policy was in her economics. She was influenced by having served as a regional councilor in an area devastated by deindustrialization whose-working class citizens felt abandoned by the major

parties in Paris. Her views were also shaped by an advisor she
hired to run her 2012 campaign. In 2009, she had met Florian
Philippot, 30, a graduate of the super-elite École nationale d'administration. (Presidents Valéry Giscard d'Estaing, Jacques
Chirac, and François Hollande were all graduates.) In 2002,
Philippot had been an enthusiastic supporter of Jean-Pierre
Chevenement, a founder of the French Socialist Party in 1969.
Chevenement had resigned from Mitterrand's cabinet in 1983
over Mitterrand's U-turn and had also opposed Maastricht and
the Euro. In 2002, he had run for President, with Philippot's
support, as the candidate of a new leftwing nationalist party
against Chirac and Hollande.

Philippot had gravitated from Chevenement's leftwing economic nationalism to the National Front by way of Jean-Yves
Gallou, a former FN member who had originally formulated its
turn toward working-class economics. In 2011, Marine Le Pen
hired Philippot to run her presidential campaign and to help
develop its platform. Its platform on economics—minus the
special preference in welfare and employment for the native
French—could have been written by Chevenement. "Jean-
Pierre Chevenement's project is carried forward by Marine Le
Pen," Philippot told *Le Monde* in 2012. As such, it was consid-
erably to the left of many of the Social Democratic or Socialist
parties on the continent and the Democratic Party in the United
States.

The platform, which is still the party's official stand, called
for a "strategic plan for reindustrialization," tariffs and quotas to
protect against "unfair competition," the separation of commercial from investment banking, a transactions tax on stock purchases, the nationalization of banks facing difficulties, a "cap"
on credit card charges, opposition to cuts in social spending
and to the privatization of public services, equal quality health

care access regardless of income or location, and rejection of the European Union's attempts to impose austerity. The EU had led, the platform said, to "open borders inducing relocation, unemployment, market dictatorship, destruction of public services, insecurity, poverty, and mass immigration." The platform blamed Greece's debt crisis on "the elites who want to feed the new Minotaur to save the Euro." The FN demanded that France's relationship to the EU be "renegotiated" and a referendum held on the Euro.

The FN's new program on economic nationalism became as integral to its appeal as its opposition to mass immigration. Its entire program was now subsumed under the concept of defending French sovereignty—in an echo of Chevenement and earlier de Gaulle, *souveraniste* was the new watchword. In Le Pen's election brochure, its position on immigration, calling for a 95 percent reduction in annual entries, came on page seven after her position on consumer rights, the Euro, jobs, finance, pensions, and justice. Together, these demands established a divide between the FN's "little people" and the establishment, which Le Pen referred to derisively (combining the UMP and PS) as the "UMPS." Le Pen insisted her own party, the FN, was not a "rightwing" party. It was *ni gauche, ni droite*, as the campaign posters proclaimed—neither left nor right. That, again, fit the populist profile.

The first test of the FN's new politics and of Le Pen as a candidate came in the 2012 presidential election. Le Pen came in third with 17.9 percent of the vote, more than her father had ever gotten in the first round. The party did well above its typical performance among 18- to 24-year-olds (26 percent), office workers (23 percent), blue-collar workers (28.6 percent), and high school graduates (27 percent). It did worst among seniors, professionals, managers, people with advanced degrees, and

Parisians. Le Pen's showing was, perhaps, helped by the public
horror over the Toulouse shootings. In its next tests, however,
it would benefit not only from new terrorist incidents, but from
the growing unpopularity of François Hollande's government.

Decline of the Socialist Party

François Hollande, France's first Socialist president since Mitterrand, assumed office in May 2012 with unemployment at 9.7
percent. In his first campaign rally, he promised to get tough
with bankers (finance is "my enemy," he proclaimed) and to
bring down France's unemployment rate. Hollande also promised to end Sarkozy and Merkel's commitment to austerity economics—dubbed "Merkozy"—and epitomized by their crafting
in 2010 an even more rigid version of the EU's Stability Pact. But
outside of a surtax on millionaires, which Hollande rescinded
after it failed to bring in significant revenue, he abandoned his
promises to break with neoliberal orthodoxy.

As unemployment rose above 10 percent, and as Hollande
was pressured by the ECB to reduce France's deficit to the 3 percent limit, he performed his own U-turn. He had already abandoned any effort to persuade Merkel to relax her support for
EU-wide adherence to the stability pact. Now having announced
that he had become a "social democrat" rather than a "socialist,"
he proposed to emulate Germany's earlier attempts to reduce
its proportion of income going to wages rather than profits by
granting business generous tax concessions, while cutting
social spending. Hollande called his new approach a *pacte de
responsabilité*—a pact of responsibility—between the government and employers. Theoretically, in exchange for these tax
concessions, business would hire more workers.

Hollande's measures alienated his own base among workers
without visibly reducing unemployment. In the first major test,

148 the municipal elections of 2014, the Socialists lost control of 113 cities and towns without winning any towns it didn't previously control. The FN did remarkably well. It got 8 percent of the total vote, even though it only ran candidates in a sixth of the municipalities. It won some important symbolic victories, including the mayor's office in Henin-Beaumont, a northern former mining town that Socialists had always controlled, and that was part of Marine Le Pen's Nord-pas-de-Calais region.

After the municipal election, Hollande replaced prime minister Jean-Marc Ayrault with Manuel Valls, who had strongly supported Hollande's U-turn. In May, however, Hollande and the PS suffered another setback. In the European parliamentary elections, Le Pen and the FN came in first with 24.85 percent, the UMP second with 20.8 percent, and Hollande's PS a distant third with 13.98 percent of the vote. The National Front did best in those blue-collar districts in the North that Socialists and Communists had once dominated. Under Hollande, the Socialists were losing what remained of their blue-collar base, but Hollande continued to meet the ECB's requirements and to emulate German labor policy.

In March 2015, Hollande unveiled new labor proposals that were reminiscent of the Hartz reforms that Schröeder had introduced in Germany in 2003. They allowed employers to pay less for overtime, and to demand more hours of work from employees; they made it easier to fire employees and limited the damages firms would have to pay for unjustified dismissals; and they allowed firms to bargain with unions for a single company rather than for a sector—a big advantage for employers, as the experience of Federal Express in the United States has shown. These proposals sparked huge demonstrations of over a million people, and *nuit debout* (up all night) demonstrations that mimicked those of the Indignados and Occupy Wall Street.

When Paris was hit with earthshaking terrorist attacks in January and November 2015. Hollande tried to take a tough line against the perpetrators. He even advanced a proposal, opposed by many in his party, that would have stripped dual citizens who committed a terrorist act of their French citizenship. But the attacks clearly boosted the FN. Wrote political scientist Pascal Perrineau, "Among the French who are deeply concerned about their safety and who also express concerns about immigration and Islam, the National Front has now reached very high levels."

In December, France held regional elections—roughly equivalent to statehouse elections in the United States. And voters once again repudiated Hollande and the PS. In the first round, Le Pen and the FN came in first with 27.73 percent, the Republicans (the successor of the UMP) second with 26.65 percent, and the PS third with 23.12 percent. In the second round, the Socialists and Republicans agreed to endorse whichever of their candidates stood the best chance of defeating the FN candidate. The strategy worked. The FN didn't win any regional presidencies, although it got almost 7 million votes and won many lesser regional offices. The Socialist Party, which had dominated regional governments, lost 15 regional presidencies.

Perrineau, using extensive polls taken immediately after ISIS attacks in November, contended that the FN was expanding beyond the small shopkeepers in the south and the blue-collar workers in the north. By his estimates, the FN was backed by 35 percent of the self-employed, 41 percent of office workers and 46 percent of blue-collar workers. In addition, FN had broken through among the public sector workers who had always been the bastion of Socialist Party support. According to Perrineau, FN was getting 30 percent of these workers, who, he explained, were reacting to "the difficulties public servants confront with immigrant people in the public hospitals and other public facilities."

Political scientist Laurent Bouvet attributed the FN's growing support among the French middle class to that class's conviction that it has to pay for—literally and figuratively—the burden migrants put on French social services. Bouvet said, "The middle class is stuck in the middle, and they have to pay for the unemployed and the migrants. The public services, the social protections, the hospitals, the universities, are falling apart. They are paying more and are getting less. And they don't see those at the top of the society making sacrifices. They can always put their children in the best schools. The parties have nothing to offer, blood and tears, more taxes, less social benefits, less jobs."

After the election, Hollande's approval rating stood at a historically low 15 percent. With the presidential elections looming in the spring of 2017, Hollande and the French Socialists were in disarray. Some Socialist Party members called for a general "primary of the left," which would include some of the smaller leftwing parties, to choose an overall candidate. Within the PS, Hollande may be challenged from both the right and the left. Frédéric Martel, a writer who is advising a candidate on the Socialist left, said, "There is nothing socialist in the Socialist Party anymore. Its base is mainly civil servants with lifetime jobs, the new bourgeois of the left, people attracted for something other than economic reasons such as gay marriage."

Party loyalists blamed Hollande's ineptitude for the Socialists' decline, but the French Socialists were following the same downward sloping path as several other Socialist, Social Democratic, and Labour parties in the EU, including PASOK in Greece and Britain's Labour Party. All these parties have had difficulty

dealing with Europe's downturn and with the Great Recession.
And in France, a clear beneficiary was the National Front.

Calm France

The question now is whether Marine Le Pen can win the 2017 presidential elections. Éric Zemmour, a conservative columnist for *Figaro* and the author of the best-selling *Suicide Fran-cais*, says, "The French elite want to push the country to be part of a European empire. The workers want to keep France national. The elite want them to forget the old France. It is a war between the elite and the people. Seventy percent of the French people want a solution against Islam and foreigners, but seventy percent don't want the National Front to come to power." When people think of the FN, Zemmour explained, they have "a fear of civil war, fear of the end of democracy, and fear of incompetence."

Zemmour's percentages may exaggerate the obstacles the FN faces in winning over a majority, but as the December regional elections showed, there are currently limits to its support, even among those who back its stands on immigration and Islam. Marine Le Pen and her circle of advisors, headed by Philippot, have sought to shift the party's emphasis away from immigration and Islam to economics and Euroskepticism. Le Pen applauded Britain's vote on leaving the EU, and called for a similar referendum in France.

When I interviewed Sébastien Chenu, who is thought to be in line to run Le Pen's presidential campaign, he said he was attracted by the party's Euroskepticism and by Le Pen's refusal to oppose gay marriage. He didn't even mention immigration or refugees until about halfway through the interview, and when I asked him specifically about the party's stand, he lamented the party's demonization on the issue. "We are not going to throw away people who are immigrants," he said. He also rejected any

152   comparison between Marine Le Pen and Donald Trump. "We don't feel close to him," he said. "Take out the T and R, and you have UMP."

But the party's active voters are still driven primarily by opposition to immigration and Islam. In February, I attended a regional convention of the FN in Henin-Beaumont and interviewed several of the local FN leaders as well as some of the rank and file. When I asked them why they had joined the FN, they invariably mentioned immigration first. Municipal councilor Antoine Golliot said, "It was the fight against immigration that was the main thing that attracted me to the FN. That is where the danger comes from." When I asked him whether the FN attracted former socialists and communists, he said, "We draw some from the right and some from the left, but overall from both sides. What draws people the most is immigration."

In the south, the party's base among small business and elderly retains the FN's older libertarian anti-tax economics and is skeptical of Philippot's leftwing nationalism. The party's Catholics in the south, including Le Pen's niece Marion Maréchal Le Pen, who is a member of parliament and the party's vice-president, are uncomfortable with Marine Le Pen's cosmopolitan outlook on abortion and gay marriage. Several of her key advisors, including Philippot and Sébastien Chenu, are gay, which prompted her father to rail against his daughter's "gay lobby." Marion Marechal Le Pen and those close to her also reject Philippot's emphasis on economic nationalism. "Unemployment is in third place behind security and identity," she has said. "A father is afraid of his daughter wearing a *burqa*. It doesn't matter whether she will buy it with francs or euros." After the Nice attack, Marine Le Pen singled out "Islamist fundamentalism," while her niece framed the issue as Christians versus Muslims. "Christians must stand up to resist Islam," she declared.

But even in the face of opposition from within, Le Pen and her advisors are determined to soften her image. In January, the FN unveiled a new campaign poster. It showed a wistful Le Pen looking out from a rural background. It was titled in large white block letters, *La France Apaisee*, meaning "Calm France" or "France Calmed Down." The poster recalls Mitterrand's 1981 poster, which read *Force Tranquille*, or a "calming force." Both posters were meant to reassure voters that the candidates were not extremists who would threaten democracy and public order.

For Le Pen, such an approach carries the risk of diluting the party's populist message and distancing herself too far from her party's base. Bouvet says, "This kind of slogan is that of a regular politician. If she starts to be the usual politician, she will lose what is interesting in her—her ability to break through to disrupt the system." But Le Pen is determined, as the 2017 presidential election nears, that the FN be seen as a "party like any other."

The Past and Future of Populism

Donald Trump's campaign in the United States, the rightwing populist parties in Europe, and even the left-center Five Star Movement have repeatedly been likened to the fascists of the 1920s. Former Labor Secretary Robert Reich titles a column, "Donald Trump: American Fascist." "Yes, Donald Trump is a fascist," Jamil Smith declares in *The New Republic*. German Finance Minister Wolfgang Schaeuble described the National Front as "not a right-wing party but . . . a fascist, extremist party." Dutch philosopher Rob Rieman accused Geert Wilders's Freedom Party of being a "fascist movement." The British *Spectator* described Beppe Grillo as "Italy's New Mussolini." Examples abound.

The term "fascism" is like the term "populism." It is hard to pick out a collection of characteristics that exclusively define a fascist movement or party. The Nazi Party scapegoated an out group—the Jews. Mussolini's fascist party did not initially single out an ethnicity or nationality. But there are certainly some resemblances between some of today's populist campaigns and some of the interwar fascists: the role of the charismatic leader (Trump, Le Pen, Wilders, Grillo); the flaunting of democratic norms (Trump); the scapegoating of an out group (Trump, Le Pen, UKIP's Farage, Wilders, the Danish People's Party). But there are two major historical differences between populism today in the United States and Western Europe and the interwar fascist movements.

First, the two original fascist parties in Italy and Germany arose in the wake of the Russian Revolution. During this period, it was widely believed that socialist and communist parties would spread the revolution westward. The fascists' and Nazis' original targets were the Socialists and Communists in their countries. Their aim was not simply to defeat these parties in elections, but to destroy them through armed struggle. The fascists and Nazis blamed democracy for encouraging the rise of these movements and while some fascists initially concealed their aims, they eventually sought to replace democracy with dictatorship.

Today's populist movements in Western Europe operate openly within the democratic electoral system. They have won power and lost it like normal parties. Those that have roots in fascism like the National Front have repudiated those roots. (There are rightwing parties in Eastern Europe and Greece that have still not distanced themselves from Europe's dark past.) While some of the parties have charismatic leaders, they don't seek to invest them with the will of the state, but merely to elect them. Grillo himself has not even run for election, and the Danish People's Party, which has no prior links to fascism, has changed its top leadership the way a conventional party would. In the United States, Trump is a one-man show whose initial target was other Republicans and who has not built a movement around himself. He has displayed anti-democratic tendencies, but they are idiosyncratic. If he has any correlate

156   in European history, it is Italy's Silvio Berlusconi, not Mussolini nor Hitler.

Second, the original fascist movements arose not only in response to revolutionary change, but also as part of the continuing struggle for imperial domination that had begun in the 1870s when the European powers accelerated the process of carving up the world into colonies, protectorates, and spheres of influence. The First World War was at least in part, as Woodrow Wilson and Vladimir Lenin separately concluded, an attempt by Germany—which equaled Britain in industry, but not in colonies—to redistribute the spoils of empire. European fascism emerged as part of an attempt by a defeated Germany to reclaim what had been taken from it at Versailles and to resume the quest for empire, and by another imperial power, Italy, to gain what it felt it had been cheated out of. Hitler wanted a Thousand Year Reich and Mussolini aspired to recreate the Roman Empire. In this sense, fascism was inherently expansionist.

The rightwing populist movements in Europe are, if anything, opposed to supranational formations. They want to reassert national control of their currency, fiscal policy, and borders. They don't like to use the term "nationalist" to describe their objectives because it suggests some links with Europe's unsavory past, in which expansionism was integral to nationalism. The National Front uses the term *souveraniste* rather than *nationaliste*. In Denmark, the People's Party's Kenneth Kristiansen Berth explained, "nationalism has a very bad tone, so we don't call ourselves nationalist, we call ourselves national." In Spain, Podemos uses the term *patriotica* rather than *nacionalista*. But in fact, as foreign policy analyst George Friedman has pointed out, these movements are nationalist *as opposed to* imperialist or globalist. In contrast to interwar fascism, they exert a centrifugal rather than centripetal force on European and global politics.

Trump, too, is a nationalist. His promise to "make America great again" does not entail reacquiring the Philippines or launching new wars of conquest. On the contrary, Trump wants to withdraw from America's overseas conflicts that don't directly threaten America and to use the country's resources instead to rebuild its infrastructure and manufacturing. He is an outspoken critic of the neo-conservatives who wanted to create a new Pax Americana in the Middle East. Domestically, Trump wants to build a wall to stop illegal immigration. He wants to strengthen America's borders not expand them.

Calling these parties and campaigns "fascist" can make for effective politics. It does bring out what is most toxic about these movements—their scapegoating of other nationalities and religions and in Trump's case, too, the encouragement of thuggery—but it is not helpful for understanding their actual role in contemporary history. Calling them fascist exaggerates the danger they pose—they don't threaten to wage war or disband parliaments. That may be the case in the future as conditions change in the U.S. or Europe, but it's not an accurate view of where they are at present. If they are repellent, it is for the *kind* of exclusionary nationalism they profess not for their global ambitions.

Populism as an Early Warning

The heated denunciation of these campaigns and parties, based on inexact historical analogies, makes it difficult to understand why what populists say resonates with the greater public, and how they are pointing, however imperfectly, to real problems that the major parties are downplaying or ignoring. By the nature of populism, these campaigns and parties point to problems through demands that are unlikely to be realized in the present political circumstances. In the case of some rightwing populists, the demands are laced with bigotry or challenge democratic norms. In other cases, they are clouded with misinformation. But they still point to tears in the fabric of accepted political wisdom.

The People's Party may have been wrong in seeing free silver as a panacea or in advancing a complex sub-treasury scheme to help farmers, but it was not wrong to decry unregulated finance and freight, growing economic inequality, and a corrupt and undemocratic political system. Long's tax schemes didn't add up, but he got the Roosevelt administration to pay attention to the maldistribution of wealth. Sanders's Medicare for all or free college may not get through a penurious Congress, and the plans themselves may need considerable tinkering, but they are arguably worthy objectives that respond to the anxiety about their situation that many Americans feel.

Trump is bloviating in threatening huge tariffs against China or against manufacturers that move their factories to Mexico, or in wanting to rip up NAFTA, but there has been a problem with American trade with China and with unfettered capital mobility. According to David Autor, David Dorn, and Gordon H. Hanson, China's imports between 1999 and 2011 cost the United States 2.4 million jobs and particularly hurt workers in the bottom 40 percent of income distribution. During the 2000s, the Commerce Department reported, American multinational corporations cut their American workforces by 2.9 million, while creating 2.4 million jobs overseas.

Syriza and Podemos might end up as "model prisoners" of Germany and the Eurozone, but they and the National Front, and the Five Star Movement have been right to point to the dysfunctionality of the EU and the Euro. In this case, one member of the Troika has come around, but it's too late. In June 2016, after Greece already lay in fiscal ruin, the IMF's journal *Finance*

& *Development* ran an essay by three of its economists entitled, "Neoliberalism: Oversold?" The economists warned that "instead of delivering growth, some neoliberal policies have increased inequality, in turn jeopardizing durable expansion." On the website Social Europe, economist Andrew Watt commented, "A definition of chutzpah is murdering your parents and then claiming social benefits as an orphan. It is not widely recognized, but the IMF illustrates similar brazenness in the current debate on Greece's debt burden."

Finally, rightwing populist campaigns and groups have held racist or nativist or xenophobic views, but their complaints point to genuine problems. George Wallace's call for segregation forever was clearly racist, but he was right about the pitfalls of busing children of different races from one urban neighborhood to another. It did result in white flight to the suburbs and was in that sense self-defeating. Trump, Buchanan, the National Front, and the Danish People's Party have courted nativist sentiments in attacking illegal and legal immigration, but they are right that unskilled immigration has tended to pull down wages and burden the public sector. Writes Cambridge University economist Ha-Joon Chang, "Wages in rich countries are determined more by immigration control than anything else, including any minimum wage legislation. How is the immigration maximum determined? Not by the 'free' labor market, which, if left alone, will end up replacing 80–90 percent of native workers with cheaper, and often more productive, immigrants."

In a deeper sense, the existence of an immigrant underclass can undermine the public trust on which a welfare state or social democracy needs to be based. Social democracy does not necessarily require ethnic homogeneity. But when ethnic heterogeneity takes the form of an immigrant underclass, then it can make citizens less willing to pay taxes to support social benefits. By the same token, as French sociologist Olivier Roy has warned, the existence in countries like France of a ghettoized underclass can also be a seedbed for political extremism and terrorism. Rightwing populists wrongly look at Islam the religion as the cause of extremism, and advocate the public suppression of Islam, but they at least acknowledge there is a problem with these communities that must be addressed.

Populism and Neoliberalism

In the United States, Trump's and Sanders's assault against the neoliberal consensus significantly shifted the economic debate during the 2016 presidential election. At the Republican and Democratic conventions, there was little mention of the supply-side nostrums that had been a staple of both parties' economics. Trump didn't waver from the stands he had taken in the primaries; and Clinton adopted much of Sanders's message. Neither candidate mentioned deficits in their speeches nor pledged to reduce what neoliberals have called "entitlements"; both pledged to be vigilant about trade deals and runaway shops; both committed themselves to regulating Wall Street. In the primaries, Sanders had been the only candidate to call for reviving the Glass-Steagall Act, but both party platforms called for reviving some version of the act.

How much this shift in debate will be reflected after the November election remains unclear. If Trump is soundly defeated, as seems likely at this writing, the Republican congressional and business leadership will argue that his defeat was due not only to his intemperate and amateurish campaigning, but to his populism. After Barry Goldwater was defeated in 1964, leading Republicans made similar arguments. But in the case of Goldwater, more polished imitators sprung up who eventually transformed the Republican Party. If

Trump's campaign does spawn imitators, the Republicans will face a continuing conflict between its white working class and business supporters.

Sanders's campaign is likely to have a more certain impact on the Democratic Party even if he himself fades from the scene. Sanders's outlook is well represented in Congress by senators Elizabeth Warren and Sherrod Brown and by the House Progressive Caucus, which Sanders helped to found. If Hillary Clinton does win the presidency, they are likely to provide a counterweight to the neoliberal influence of Wall Street and Silicon Valley among the Democrats. That should lead to continuing conflict within the party.

In the near term, however, the United States is not likely to experience a political earthquake that would overturn neoliberalism and realign the parties. American neoliberalism has been based on an implicit global arrangement in which the United States runs large trade deficits, particularly to countries in Asia, and the countries send back the dollars from their trade surpluses to fund our deficits and fuel consumer demand. That arrangement could fray and precipitate a crisis, but it remains semi-intact for the moment. The American workforce will continue to skew away from the middle, but as long as those in the middle can still find work, a crisis is unlikely. Also, the United States is in a better position than Europe to control its flow of immigrants, including unauthorized immigrants. What is happening is an erosion rather than a disintegration of the neoliberal agenda.

But in the words of Herbert Stein, things that can't go on forever, don't. The circulatory system of trade deficits, recycled dollars, and private and public debt that sustains neoliberalism won't go on forever, and when it does cease, or fray to the point of breaking, there will be a reckoning for which the Perot,

162 Buchanan, Sanders, and Trump campaigns will have prepared the way.

Europe is another matter entirely. The European Union and the Eurozone were built with the best of intentions, but many Europeans have not seen their benefits, particularly those who live in the less prosperous nations within the Eurozone. The case against the Euro is not new. It was stated clearly by economist Wynne Godley in the *London Review of Books* in 1992:

> What happens if a whole country—a potential 'region' in a fully integrated community—suffers a structural setback? So long as it is a sovereign state, it can devalue its currency. It can then trade successfully at full employment provided its people accept the necessary cut in their real incomes. With an economic and monetary union, this recourse is obviously barred, and its prospect is grave indeed unless federal budgeting arrangements are made which fulfill a redistributive role.

And of course, no federal budgeting arrangements were made. Fiscal policy, and the revenues on which it is based have remained in national hands, and to make matters worse, the Stability and Growth Pact—and its 2012 successor, the Stability Pact—have drastically limited the use of deficit spending to ease unemployment. If the EU were to move toward a centralized fiscal and monetary policy, as Varoufakis and other left-wing economists have proposed, then the Eurocrisis could be eased, but there is huge resistance to doing that, particularly in wealthier northern European countries, including Germany, Holland, and Finland. As a result, the prognosis for the Eurozone is negative.

And the EU's other source of disunion—the flood of asylum seekers from the Middle East and North Africa and from the poorer parts of the EU itself to the more prosperous—is integrally

related to the Eurocrisis. Part of the logic of open borders was that
if people in one country couldn't find jobs they could move to
another. Large-scale immigration is the price that northern European countries have had to pay for their success, and it's a major
reason for Britain's voting to leave the EU. It has fueled rightwing populism *and* adamant opposition among groups like the
True Finns, the Danish People's Party, the Dutch Freedom Party,
and the Alternative fur Deutschland to any federal budgeting
arrangements that fulfill a redistributive role.

Some experts on European politics, including Oxford political scientist Jan Zielonka, think that the EU is destined to disintegrate. That's beyond my own power of speculation. But I
think it is fair to say that the pressures that have created rightwing and leftwing populist parties in Europe will, if anything,
grow, and could reach the point where several other countries
besides Great Britain decide to bolt. If that happens, the EU,
which Barack Obama called "one of the greatest achievements
of modern times," will suffer the fate that former, and far less
benign, attempts at a European confederation have suffered.

ACKNOWLEDGMENTS

I want to thank Nick Lemann, Jimmy So, and Camille McDuffie of Columbia Global Reports for their help, advice, support, and encouragement in getting this book done, and my agent Rafe Sagalyn for suggesting to me that I do a book with them. Larry Lynn, Arthur Goldhammer, Thomas Edsall, David Peck, Joan Pedro Caranana, Jørgen Dragsdahl and James Shoch read all or parts of the manuscript, and told me when they thought I had gone astray. Needless to say, they are not to blame for whatever errors or misinterpretations I've made but I would have had a hard time without their help. I talked about many of the ideas with Michael Lind. I was also aided in the United States on specific points and on suggestions for what I should read and whom I should see by Christopher Caldwell, Theda Skocpol, Cas Mudde, Sidney Blumenthal, and James Galbraith. In France, I got assistance in understanding the politics and making contacts from Frédéric Martel, Anne-Elizabeth Moutet, Nonna Mayer, and Marianne Niosi. In Spain, I enjoyed the hospitality of David Peck and Susanne Mack, and David was my expert guide and advisor. I also got help from Laura Tedesco, Maria Del Val Gomez, Daniel Inerrarity, and Michael Tangeman. In Denmark, I was advised by my old friend Jørgen Dragsdahl. And I was also aided by Martin Burcharth, Anders Pedersen, and Susi Meret. At the library of the Carnegie Endowment in Washington, Kathleen Higgs, Keigh Hammond, and Christopher Lao-Scott got me the books I needed to consult. I am eternally grateful to my wife, Susan Pearson, and to my daughters, Eleanor and Hilary, for their advice, encouragement, and forbearance.

I argue in *The Populist Explosion* that there is a significant strain of politics widely called "populist" that appeared in the United States in the 1880s and in Europe in the 1970s, and that it is different from conventional American liberalism, conservatism, European social democracy, and Christian democracy. In analyzing how it works, I was influenced by the late Ernesto Laclau's book, *On Populist Reason* (Verso, 2005). Laclau portrays populism as a *logic* that can be used by the left as well as the right, and he explains how the demands that populists make are different from those of other parties and candidates. There is also a useful anthology, *Populism and the Mirror of Democracy* (Verso, 2005), edited by Francisco Panizza, which includes essays by Laclau and Chantal Mouffe. Laclau's essay, "Populism: What's in a Name?" is a remarkably clear summary of his thesis, and Mouffe's "The 'End of Politics' and the Challenge of Right-wing Populism" counters the usual dismissal of populism by European intellectuals and politicians. (For a further discussion of Laclau and Mouffe, see my own essay on them in *Dissent*, Fall 2016.)

American historians have recognized that populism can appear on the left or right, from the People's Party to George Wallace. Michael Kazin's *The Populist Persuasion* (Basic Books, 1995) reflects this understanding. Kazin's treatment of populism as a "language" is similar to Laclau's view of it as a "logic." Most European studies focus on rightwing populism. That's partly because populist parties initially arose on the right there. And perhaps because of the memory of Hitler and Mussolini, many of these studies see Western European populism as a threat to democracy. I found Cas Mudde's *Populist Radical Right Parties in Europe* (Cambridge University Press, 2007) useful. I also liked Christopher Caldwell's *Reflections on the Revolution in Europe: Immigration, Islam and the West* (Anchor, 2009) as well as his essays on European populism in the *Weekly Standard*.

The key book to understanding American rightwing populism, from George Wallace through Donald Trump, is Donald I. Warren's

166 *The Radical Center: Middle Americans and the Politics of Alienation* (University of Notre Dame Press, 1976). Warren, a largely unheralded sociologist who taught at Oakland University in Michigan, conducted extensive surveys of Wallace voters in the early 1970s. Warren discovered a strain of politics that blended right and left, which he called "middle American radicalism." It endures in Trump's support. Kevin Phillips is another invaluable analyst of American populism, from *The Emerging Republican Majority* (Arlington House, 1969) to *Arrogant Capital: Washington, Wall Street, and the Frustration of American Politics* (Little Brown, 1994). On Huey Long, I relied on Alan Brinkley's *Voices of Protest: Huey Long, Father Coughlin, and the Great Depression* (Knopf, 1982). On the Tea Party, I found Theda Skocpol and Vanessa Williamson's *The Tea Party and the Remaking of Republican Conservatism* (Oxford University Press, 2012) useful, as well a doctoral thesis by Emily Elisabeth Ekins, "Tea Party Fairness: How the Idea of Proportional Justice Explains the Right-Wing Populism of the Obama Era." (http://escholarship.org/uc/item/3663x343)

In describing the economic roots and ideology of neoliberalism, I was influenced by Robert Brenner's *The Economics of Global Turbulence* (Verso, 2006). The crucial role played by Margaret Thatcher and François Mitterrand is described by Peter Hall in *Governing the Economy: The Politics of State Intervention in Britain and France* (Oxford University Press, 1986). In analyzing the Eurocrisis and the onset of the Great Recession in Europe, I was also influenced by Hall's more recent work, particularly an essay, "Varieties of Capitalism and the Eurocrisis," in *West European Politics*, August 2014. I first became aware that the adoption of the Euro was leading Europe into a cul-de-sac thanks to Paul Krugman's columns in *The New York Times*. I became convinced of the special role played by German export surpluses from the "Appendix" to Michael Pettis's book, *The Great Rebalancing: Trade, Conflict, and the Perilous Road Ahead for the World Economy* (Princeton University Press, 2013). Pettis also has an interesting essay on Greece, Spain, and the Eurozone crisis, "Syriza and the French Indemnity of 1871–73," on his blog (http://blog.mpettis.com/2015/02/syriza-and-the-french-indemnity-of-1871-73/). For other relevant books and articles, see my endnotes.

In following European Union politics, I found two websites invaluable: Social Europe (socialeurope.eu) and Open Democracy (opendemocracy.net). Arthur Goldhammer keeps up with "French politics" (artgoldhammer.blogspot.com) and Michael Tangeman with Spain (progressivespain.com). One of the best sources on left-wing populism in Greece and Spain is the *New Left Review*. Podemos's leader Pablo Iglesias was interviewed in the publication's May–June 2015 issue. The party's chief strategist Íñigo Errejón also conducted a dialogue about populist politics with Chantal Mouffe in the book *Podemos: In the Name of the People* (Lawrence & Wishart, 2016). I also benefited from James Galbraith's analyses of the Greek crisis, which was summed up in his recent book, *Welcome to the Poisoned Chalice: The Destruction of Greece and the Future of Europe* (Yale University Press, 2016).

INTRODUCTION

13   well ahead in polls: "https://
www.noties.nl/v/get.php?a=peil
.nl&s=weekpoll&f=De+Stemming+
van+10+januari+2016. pdf

14   exclusively in all of them:
For this analysis of language, see
Ludwig Wittgenstein, *Philosophi-
cal Investigations*, Basil Blackwell,
1953, Part I. For political language,
the lack of an "essence" is even
more obvious if you think of terms
like "liberal" and "conservative,"
and their very different use from
country to country.

14   and Spain's Podemos: My
own analysis of populism has been
heavily influenced by, but is still
somewhat different from, that of
Ernesto Laclau, *On Populist Reason*,
Verso, 2005.

14   former against the latter:
Michael Kazin, *The Populist Per-
suasion: An American History*, Basic
Books, 1995, p. 1.

CHAPTER ONE

18   nomination in 2016: http://
www.xojane.com/issues/stephanie-
cegielski-donald-trump-
campaign-defector

18   downscale white Americans:
See http://www.politico.com/
magazine/story/2016/01/donald-
trump-2016-authoritarian-2135
33#ixzz43pWmnAgK and http://
www.slate.com/articles/news_and_
politics/cover_story/2016/03/how_
donald_trump_happened_racism_
against_barack_obama.html

18   weakness as a frontrunner:
See http://www.bloombergview
.com/articles/2016-02-01/what-
bernie-sanders-gets-about-
millennials.

21   the legend goes: McMath,
p. 75.

22   the gold standard: Robert C.
McMath, Jr., *American Populism: A
Social History 1877-1898*, Hill and
Wang, 1992, p. 146.

24   as "bourgeois": Charles
Postel, *The Populist Vision*, Oxford
University Press, 2007, p. 208.

24   John J. Ingalls wrote: McMath,
op. cit., p. 135.

**25   "second Declaration of Inde-
pendence":** Postel, op. cit., p. 158.

25   "cease in the land": *The
Populist Mind*, ed. Norman Pollack,
Bobbs-Merrill, 1967, pp. 61—63.

26   "despotism, and death?": *The
Populist Mind*, p. 46.

26   "moral and social lepers":
Postel, p. 185.

**26   "Anarchists, and Commu-
nists":** McMath, p. 69.

26   "farmer deserves none":
McMath, p. 182.

27   "one word—nigger": McMath,
p. 173.

27   "foreign pauper labor":
http://www.presidency.ucsb.edu/
ws/?pid=29586

30   "the people" together: On
Long's life and politics, see T. Harry
Williams, *Huey Long*, Knopf, 1969.

Alan Brinkley, *Voices of Protest: Huey Long, Father Coughlin, and the Great Depression*, Knopf, 1982.

30 **"the ground he walks on":** Brinkley, p. 29.

30 **"Mr. Rockefeller":** Brinkley, p. 59.

30 **what he promised:** Brinkley, pp. 72–73.

30 **"base your conclusions?":** Michael Hiltzik, *The New Deal: A Modern History*, Free Press, 2011, p. 221.

31 **more than 7.5 million:** William Leuchtenberg, *Franklin Roosevelt and the New Deal*, Harpercollins, 1963, p. 99.

31 **politically volatile group:** Brinkley, p. 198.

31 **to the Republicans:** Leucthenberg, pp. 99–100.

31 **Long had repeatedly raised:** On whether Roosevelt and the Democrats in Congress were responding to Long and Coughlin, see Brinkley, pp. 79–81. Or Alonzo Hamby, *Man of Destiny: FDR and the Making of the American Century*, Basic Books, 2015, p. 238.

32 **"soaking the rich":** Frank Freidel, *Franklin D. Roosevelt: A Rendezvous with Destiny*, Back Bay Books, 1990, pp. 165–66.

32 **"economic royalists":** http://www.austincc.edu/lpatrick/his2341/fdr36acceptancespeech.htm

33 **outniggered again:** Marshall Frady, *Wallace*, New York, Dutton, 1968, p. 127. Wallace denied using the exact phrase, and another fellow politician said he used "out-segged." Stephan Lesher, *George Wallace: American Populist*, Perseus Books, 1994, p. 129.

34 **the little businessman:** Lesher, p. 390.

34 **fleeing to Virginia:** http://www.ourcampaigns.com/CandidateDetail.html?CandidateID=4038.

34 **welfare, roads, and agriculture:** http://www.4president.org/brochures/wallace1968brochure.htm.

35 **"without paying taxes":** Lesher, p. 474.

35 **"punks were in diapers":** http://www.ourcampaigns.com/CandidateDetail.html?CandidateID=4038.

35 **"rich and poor simultaneously":** Donald I. Warren, *The Radical Center*, University of Notre Dame Press, 1976. p. 20.

35 **"have to pay the bill":** Warren, p. 21.

35 **"too big":** Warren, p. 73.

36 **George Wallace in 1972:** Warren, p. 151.

36 **Warren's MARs:** Irving Crespi, "Structural Sources of the George Wallace Constituency," *Social Science Quarterly*, June 1971.

CHAPTER TWO

40 **free market liberalism:** There is a controversy about the use of the term "neoliberalism" that I

170   would prefer to avoid. See http://
coreyrobin.com/tag/neoliberalism/
In the U.S. there are at least three
uses of the term: 1) post-New Deal
liberalism championed by Charles
Peters of the *Washington Monthly*
and his protégés that is wary of
"big labor" and "big government"
solutions and prefers means-test-
ed over universal social programs.
2) Gary Hart's politics of 1984—88
that stressed achieving growth
rather than equity through the
use of an industrial policy that
targeted high-tech industries;
and 3) the dominance of Reagan's
Republicanism that accepted the
existence of the safety net, but
sought to lower taxes on business,
remove regulations, free capital to
move overseas, and allow immigrants to move into the United
States. Democrats, including Bill
Clinton, would accept some qual-
ified version of this third version,
as Labor's Tony Blair's New Labour
would accept some version of Margaret Thatcher's neoliberalism. It's
the third kind of neoliberalism to
which I am referring in this book.

41   **automobiles, and refrigerators:** On global overcapacity in the
'70s and beyond, see *The International Politics of Surplus Capaci-
ty,* ed. Susan Strange and Roger
Tooze, Routledge, 1981.

41   **23.1 percent in non-
manufacturing:** See Robert
Brenner, *The Economics of Global
Turbulence,* Verso, 2006, pp. 108—9
and Leo Panitch and Sam Gindin,
*The Making of Global Capitalism:
The Political Economy of American
Empire,* Verso, 2012, p. 135.

41   **rates of profit:** For the "profit
squeeze" theory that rising wage
and benefit costs drove the neoliberal reaction, the classic explanation is Andrew Glyn and Robert
Sutcliffe, *British Capitalism, Workers and the Profit Squeeze,* Penguin
Books, 1972. Several economists
applied this analysis to the U.S.
For a recent example, see Panitch
and Gindin, op. cit. The overcapacity and profit squeeze theses are
sometimes presented as alternative explanations, but I think
they both describe pressures that
resulted in the end of the postwar
boom in the U.S. and Europe.

41   **"labor unions, and the
young":** John B. Judis, *The Paradox
of American Democracy,* Pantheon,
2000, p. 11.

41   **American firms from expropriation:** I describe business's new
lobbying offensive in *The Paradox
of American Democracy,* Chapter
Five.

42   **plants were undocumented:**
The New York Times, December
12, 2001. In addition, immigration also exacted a cost in welfare
spending for cities, states, and the
federal government. According to
a Center for Immigration Studies
analysis, in 2012, between 62 and
65.6 percent of illegal immigrants
received some kind of welfare assistance compared to 48.5 percent
of legal immigrant households and
only 30.2 percent of native-born
households.

43   **38 percent for:** http://articles.
latimes.com/1993-11-09/news/
mn-54845_1_gallup-poll.

43   **32 percent for:** http://www
.pipa.org/OnlineReports/
Globalization/Americans
Globalization_Mar00/Americans
Globalization_Mar00_apdxa.pdf.

43   **"big government":** See
Kevin Phillips, *Arrogant Capital:
Washington, Wall Street, and the
Frustration of American Politics,*
Little Brown, 1994.

45   **rise in inequality:** See John H.
Dunn, Jr. "The Decline of
Manufacturing in the United
States, and Its Impact on Income
Inequality," *The Journal of Applied
Business Research,* September–
October 2012.

45   **white-collar jobs:** Peter
Temin, "The American Dual Econ-
omy," *Institute for New Economic
Thinking,* November 2015.

45   **bottom 70 percent:** http://
www.urban.org/research/
publication/growing-size-and-
incomes-upper-middle-class.

46   **wrong with the U.S. economy:**
Daniel Yankelovich, "Foreign Policy
after the Election," *Foreign Affairs,*
Fall 1992.

47   **obtaining an early discharge:**
On Perot's life, see Gerald Posner,
Citizen Perot: His Life and Times,
Random House, 1996.

47   **GM's management ignored
him:** See Doron P. Levin, *Irrecon-
cilable Differences: Ross Perot Versus
General Motors,* Little Brown, 1989.

48   **it's going to be too late:**
Address to National Press Club,
March 18, 1992.

49   **make America work again:**
Ross Perot, *Ross Perot: My Life and
the Principles for Success,* Tapestry
Press, 2002, p. 99.

49   **"industries of the future":**
Ross Perot, p. 61.

49   **"biogenetics industry":** Ibid.

49   **"dictatorial":** Stanley Green-
berg, *The Road to Realignment: the
Democrats and the Perot Voters,*
Democratic Leadership Council,
1993, pp. II-9.

50   **had a chance to win:** Posner,
p. 322.

50   **as liberal or conservative:**
Frank Luntz, "Perovian Civiliza-
tion," *Policy Review,* Spring 1993.

50   **"the radical middle":** Green-
berg, pp. II-3.

50   **"worse now than in 1988":**
http://www.cnn.com/ELECTION/
1998/states/CA/polls/CA92PH
.html.

50   **"a raw deal today":** Green-
berg, p. III-11.

51   **trade loses more jobs:** Cited
in Ruy Teixeira and Guy Molyneux, *Economic Nationalism and
the Future of American Politics,*
Economic Policy Institute. 1993,
p. 29.

51   **"tougher U.S. trade stance":**
Teixeira and Molyneux, p. 24.

51   **"rob us of American jobs":**
Washington Post, September 9,
1991. John B. Judis, "The Tariff
Party," *The New Republic,* March
30, 1992.

172

52 **"if not for its people?":** Buchanan, *Pittsburgh Post-Gazette,* November 28, 1995.

52 **"Robert Rubin's world":** Buchanan, *Arizona Republic,* February 9, 1995.

52 **"isn't really a country anymore":** John B. Judis, "Taking Pat Buchanan Seriously," *GQ,* December 1995.

52 **"peasants with pitchforks":** Tom Raum, "Leading a Revolution of Peasants with Pitchforks," Associated Press, February 18, 1996.

53 **real income had begun to rise:** https://www.census.gov/hhes/www/income/data/incpovhlth/1996/highlights.html.

54 **A steep recession followed:** John B. Judis, "Debt Man Walking," *The New Republic,* December 3, 2008, and Michael Pettis, *The Great Rebalancing: Trade, Conflict and the Perilous Road Ahead for the World Economy,* Princeton University Press, 2013.

54 **had backed McGovern in 1972:** See John B. Judis and Ruy Teixeira, *The Emerging Democratic Majority,* New York, 2002.

54 **new enduring Democratic majority:** John B. Judis, "America the Liberal," *The New Republic,* Nov. 19, 2008.

55 **prepare the nation for a new age:** https://www.whitehouse.gov/blog/2009/01/21/president-barack-obamas-inaugural-address.

55 **did not prosecute:** http://www.g-a-i.org/u/2012/08/DOJ-Report-8-61.pdf.

55 **shake business confidence:** See Noam Scheiber, *The Escape Artists: How Obama's Team Fumbled the Recovery,* Simon & Schuster, 2011, pp. 170–8.

55 **growth of Medicare spending:** See Thomas B. Edsall, "The Obamacare Crisis," *The New York Times,* November 19, 2013 and "Is Obamacare Destroying the Democratic Party," *The New York Times,* December 2, 2014.

56 **"Chicago Tea Party":** See John B. Judis, "Tea Minus Zero," *The New Republic,* May 10, 2010.

56 **160,000 members:** Theda Skocpol and Vanessa Williamson, *The Tea Party and the Remaking of Republican Conservatism,* Oxford University Press, 2012, p. 22.

57 **"You are not entitled to what I have earned":** Skocpol and Williamson, p. 66.

57 **ACA as a redistributive transfer program:** Emily Elisabeth Ekins, "Tea Party Fairness: How the Idea of Proportional Justice Explains the Right-Wing Populism of the Obama Era," UCLA diss., 2015, pp. 74–75.

57 **services by illegal immigrants:** Skocpol and Williamson, p. 71.

57 **took jobs from native-born Americans:** See Kazin, pp. 35–36.

58 **sending him big checks:** John B. Judis, "David Brat and the

Triumph of Rightwing Populism," *The New Republic*, June 11, 2014.

59 **from 2007 through 2011:** http://www2.itif.org/2015-inequality-rose.pdf

59 **some college or a bachelor's degree:** https://web.stanford.edu/group/recessiontrends/cgi-bin/web/sites/all/themes/barron/pdf/LaborMarkets_fact_sheet.pdf

59 **"The Economic Elite vs. the People of the United States":** For AmpedStatus.com's role see http://www.washingtonsblog.com/2011/09/a-report-from-the-frontlines-the-long-road-to-occupywallstreet-and-the-origins-of-the-99-movement.html. On the history of Occupy Wall Street, see Todd Gitlin, *Occupy Nation: The Roots, the Spirit, and the Promise of Occupy Wall Street*, It Books, 2012; Ethan Earle, *A Brief History of Occupy Wall Street*, Rosa Luxemburg Stiftung, 2012; Mattathias Schwartz, "Pre-Occupied," *The New Yorker*, November 28, 2011.

61 **finally undid it:** Jonathan Mahler, "Oakland, the Last Refuge of Radical America," *New York Times*, August 1, 2012.

CHAPTER THREE

62 **"protest candidate":** https://www.washingtonpost.com/news/post-politics/wp/2015/07/03/bernie-sanders-seen-as-a-protest-candidate-says-democratic-rival-martin-omalley/.

62 **"Trump's campaign is a sideshow":** http://www.huffingtonpost.com/entry/a-note-about-our-coverage-of-donald-trumps-campaign_us_55a8fc9ce4b0896514d0fd66?-section=politics.

62 **back into their politics section:** http://www.huffingtonpost.com/arianna-huffington/a-note-on-trump_b_8744476.html.

63 **"personality not substance":** http://www.nytimes.com/2015/08/23/us/politics/why-donald-trump-wont-fold-polls-and-people-speak.html.

63 **"Sanders's authenticity":** Pablo Zevallos, *Politico*, February 12, 2016.

64 **recouped his losses:** Michael D'Antonio, *Never Enough: Donald Trump and the Pursuit of Success*, Thomas Dunne Books, 2015.

65 **"I'm very pro-choice":** "Inside Politics," CNN, October 26, 1999.

65 **"liberal on health":** Trump and Dave Shiflett, *The America We Deserve*, Renaissance Books, 2000, p. 212.

66 **"rebuild our own country":** http://www.npr.org/2016/04/01/472633800/4-things-to-know-about-donald-trumps-foreign-policy-approach.

66 **criticized NATO:** http://www.realclearpolitics.com/video/2016/03/27/trump_europe_is_not_safe_lots_of_the_free_world_has_become_weak.html.

67 **"police that deal":** http://www.slate.com/articles/news_and_politics/politics/2016/01/donald_

174   trump_is_the_only_serious_
gop_candidate_who_hasn_t_
promised_to_rip.html.

67   **"a bunch of saps":** Associated
Press, December 2, 1999.

68   **"political hacks":** Debate,
June 28, 2015.

69   **"It's rigged against you":**
https://www.donaldjtrump.com/
press-releases/donald-j.-trump-
on-the-stakes-of-the-election.

70   **"Enter by the law, or leave":**
Trump, *The America We Deserve*,
p. 243.

70   **"Illegal immigration is a
wrecking ball":** Trump, *Time to
Get Tough*, Regnery Publishing,
2015

71   **"anti-elite party of the working class":** D'Antonio.

72   **"two Ivy League contenders":** Trump, "What I Saw at the
Revolution," *New York Times*, Feb.
19, 2000.

72   **"trying to stop me":** http://
www.msnbc.com/msnbc/donald-
trump-hammers-home-anti-
establishment-message.

72   **didn't necessarily believe:**
Mary Jordan, "A Village named
Syria in the Heart of Virginia
explains why many will vote for
Trump," *Washington Post*, May 24,
2016. Jordan writes, "Several people said that it made little sense to
pay attention too closely to elec-
tion-year proposals because candidates rarely deliver when they are
in office, especially if Congress is
needed to approve a new measure.

Richards, for instance, said she
doesn't think a ban will occur, just
as she knows that Mexico probably
won't pay for the giant wall Trump
talks about building on the southern border. But she said that no
other candidate is telling her what
she thinks: Just about anybody can
set foot in the United States, and
those days should end."

74   **"a widespread global depression":** http://www.cnbc.
com/2016/06/29/gop-donor-paul-
singer-says-trump-would-cause-
a-depression.html.

75   **The American National
Election Studies:** http://www.
electionstudies.org/

75   **Pew Research Center in
March:** http://www.people-press.
org/files/2016/03/3-31-16-March-
Political-release-1.pdf

75   **leaving the Democrats in
the '60s:** Some statistical sites
claimed that Trump's supporters
were not really "working class"
because on some exit polls, they
had an average income of $72,000,
which is above the median income.
But the principal test of whether
someone is working class or above
is usually education, and Trump's
support is inversely related to the
level of a voter's education. He
does best among high school grads
and voters with only some college.
But his support is also proportional to age, and annual income rises
with age, so the fact that Trump's
supporters have a slightly above
average income probably reflects
their age rather than their social
class.

77 **"that are angry":** http://www.bloomberg.com/features/2016-reince-priebus/. On Sanders's life story, see John B. Judis, "The Bern Supremacy," *National Journal*, November 19, 2015; Harry Jaffe, *Why Bernie Sanders Matters*, Regan Arts, 2015; Tim Murphy, "How Bernie Sanders Learned to Be a Real Politician," *Mother Jones*, May 26, 2015; and Simon van Zuylen-Wood, "I'm Right and Everybody Else Is Wrong," *National Journal*, June 2014.

79 **"nobody in the audience fainted":** Sanders, "Fragments of a Campaign Diary," *Seven Days*, December 1, 1972.

79 **"Why Socialism":** Albert Einstein, "Why Socialism," *Monthly Review*, May 1949.

79 **"I don't have the power to nationalize the banks":** *Baltimore Sun*, December 23, 1981.

79 **"I'm a democratic socialist":** Sanders with Huck Gutman, *Outsider in the House*, Verso, 1997, p. 29.

80 **higher standard of living:** Michael Powell, "Exceedingly Social, but Doesn't Like Parties," *Washington Post*, November 5, 2006.

80 **"two percent of the people":** *Saint Albans Daily Messenger*, December 23, 1971.

81 **"buy the United States Congress":** "The Rachel Maddow Show," MSNBC, April 15, 2015.

81 **"What Bernie Sanders Doesn't Understand About American Politics:"** Jonathan Chait, "What Bernie Sanders Doesn't Understand About American Politics," *New York*, January 27, 2016.

81 **"facile calls for revolution:"** "It Was Better to Bern Out," *The New York Times*, June 10, 2016.

82 **"eat out the heart of the republic":** George E. Mowry, *The Era of Theodore Roosevelt*, Harper and Brothers, 1958, p. 101.

85 **84 percent from 2008 to 2014:** Judis, "The Bern Supremacy."

85 **among college students:** Abby Holterman, "Mental Health Problems for College Students Are Increasing," *Healthline*, July 17, 2015.

85 **42 to 34 percent:** https://today.yougov.com/news/2016/01/28/democrats-remain-divided-socialism/.

86 **survive the 2016 election:** Harold Meyerson, "The Long March of Bernie's Army," *American Prospect*, Spring 2016.

CHAPTER FOUR

88 **"three destroyers":** Jim Yardley, "Europe on the March," *New York Times*, May 24, 2014.

89 **"Henk and Ingrid":** *The Changing Faces of Populism: Systemic Challenges in Europe and the U.S.*, ed. Hedwig Guisto, Stefano Rizzo, David Kitching, Lexington Books, 2013, p. 183.

89 **"demagogy, charismatic leadership":** Cas Mudde, "Populism in Europe: A Primer," *Open Democracy*, May 12, 2015.

176   89   **"Exposing the Demagogues":**
Eds. Karsten Grabow and Florian
Hartleb, *Exposing the Demagogues:
Right-wing and National Populist Parties in Europe*, Center for
European Studies, 2013. In spite
of its incendiary title, the book
contains useful scholarly studies
of Europe's populist parties.

90   **"virtuous circle":** J. Bradford
DeLong, "Post WWII European
Exceptionalism: The Economic Di-
mension," NBER, December 1997.

91   **Comparing the period 1950
to 1973:** Nicholas Crafts, "Fif-
ty Years of Economic Growth in
Western Europe," Stanford Institute for Economic Policy Research,
November 2003.

91   **a lowly 1.6 percent:** Eric
Hobsbawm, *The Age of Extremes:
A History of the World, 1914-1991,*
Pantheon Books, 1994. p. 406. My
account of Thatcher and Mitterrand's policy experiments has been
heavily influenced by Peter Hall,
*Governing the Economy: The Politics
of State Intervention in Britain and
France*, Oxford University Press,
1986.

93   **"initial decline from 1979–
81":** Tony Judt, *Postwar: A History
of Europe Since 1945*, Penguin
Books, 2006, p. 542.

95   **"to change their minds":**
http://conservativehome.blogs.
com/centreright/2008/04/
making-history.html.

96   **actively recruiting guest
workers:** For these figures, see
Stephen Castles, "The Guest
Worker in Western Europe—An

Obituary," *The International Migration Review*, Winter 1986.

96   **3.4 million in France:**
Hans-Georg Betz, *Radical Right-
Wing Populism in Western Europe*,
Palgrave Macmillan, 1994, p. 73-4.

97   **numbers have continued to
grow:** Hans-George Betz, "The
New Politics of Resentment," *Comparative Politics*, July 1993.

97   **by 268,902, or 520 percent:**
http://www.migrationpolicy.org/
article/denmark-integrating-
immigrants-homogeneous-
welfare-state.

97   **by 1991, it was 33 percent:**
Eurobarometer, June 1991, Brussels.

98   **took jobs away from natives:**
John Sides and Jack Citrin, "Euro-
pean Opinions about Immigration,"
British Journal of Political Science,
July 2007.

98   **Mogens Glistrup founded
in 1973:** Susi Meret, "The Danish
People's Party, the Italian Northern
League and the Austrian Freedom
Party in a Comparative Perspec-
tive: Party Ideology and Electoral
Support," Aalborg University, diss.
2010.

100   **"the most immigrant-
obsessed party in Europe":** Christopher Caldwell, *Reflections on the
Revolution in Europe: Immigration,
Islam and the West*, Anchor, 2009,
p. 316.

101   **"The gap was taken up by
Søren Krarup":** Interview with
author. On Krarup, I have relied
on Susi Meret, op. cit., author's
interview with Krarup's biographer

Mikael Jalving, and John Terrell Foor, "State of Identity: National History and Exclusive Identity in Contemporary Denmark," Western Michigan University MA thesis.

101   **"Your Denmark"**: translation by Cecillie Felicia Stokholm Banke.

101   **"You are not house-trained"**: Translation by Jørgen Dragsdahl. Text can be found at http://www.stm.dk/_p_7628.html

102   **inciting racial hatred:** Cas Mudde, *The Ideology of the Extreme Right*, Manchester University Press, 2000, Chapter Five. See also Paul Lucardie and Gerrit Voerman, "Geert Wilders and the Party for Freedom," *Exposing the Demagogues*.

104   **by 1999, 47 percent were:** See Reinhard Heinsich, "Austrian Right-Wing Populism," in *Exposing the Demagogues*, and Karl Aiginger, "The Privatization Experiment in Austria," *Austrian Economic Quarterly*, 4/1999.

105   **"irrational shifts in the market":** Cited in Donald A. Hempson Jr., "European Disunion: The Rise and Fall of a Post-war Dream," *Origins*, September 2013.

107   **"closed world of chancelleries":** Perry Anderson, *The New Old World*, Verso, 2009, p. 62.

107   **"The European Union will remain utopia":** Cas Mudde, *Populist Radical Right Parties in Europe*, Cambridge University Press, 2007, p. 159.

107   **"a new European superstate is not":** Mudde, p. 166.

CHAPTER FIVE   177

110   **25.1 percent in 2012:** http://www.economicshelp.org/blog/1247/economics/european-unemployment- 2/

110   **cause of the deepening recession:** There is now an extensive literature on the causes of the Eurocrisis, and the explanation I offer here is a hybrid of several. See Peter A. Hall, "Varieties of Capitalism and the Eurocrisis," *West European Politics*, August 2014; Heiner Flassback and Kostas Lapavitsas, *Against the Troika: Crisis and Austerity in the Eurozone*, Verso, 2015; Engelbert Stockhammer, "The Euro Crisis and the Contradictions of Neoliberalism in Europe," *Post Keynesian Economics Study Group*, Working Paper 1401; Mark Copelovtich, Jeffry Frieden, and Stefanie Walter, "The Political Economy of the Euro Crisis," *Comparative Political Studies*, 2016; Servaas Storm and C. W. Naastepad, "Myths, Mixups, and Mishandlings: Understanding the Eurozone Crisis," *International Journal of Political Economy* 45, 2016; and Pettis, op. cit., Appendix.

For a narrative of the events, see Stathis Kouvelakis, "The Greek Cauldron," *New Left Review*, November–December 2011.

112   **"treasonous":** Ibid.

113   **Greece will be massively limited:** http://globalcomment.com/loansharking-greece-Syriza-the-troika-and-the-end-of-greek-sovereignty/.

114 member of the European community: For this history of Syriza, see Yanis Varoufakis, "Can Greece's Syriza Change Europe's Economy," *Boston Review*, December 3, 2013.

115 rural voters: Yiannis Mavris, "Greece's Austerity Election," *New Left Review*, July–August 2012.

116 "the Greece of Democracy": Yannis Stavrakakis and Giorgos Katsambakis, "Leftwing Populism in the European Periphery: the case of Syriza," *Journal of Political Ideologies*, 2014. The authors have precisely enumerated Tsipras's use of populist terms in his speeches.

116 "acting like a model prisoner": Varoufakis, op. cit.

117 "the Troika is over": Euractiv, February 12, 2015.

117 "it wasn't the Greeks who did it": Paul Krugman, "Killing the European Project," *The New York Times*, July 12, 2015.

117 simply appalling: Flassbeck and Lapavitsas.

118 Berlin finance ministry: Interview with author.

119 "A rupture is indispensable": Interview with Stathis Kouvelakis, *New Left Review*, January–February 2016.

119 "Spain is the problem, and Europe is the solution": Cited in Omar G. Encarnacion, *Spanish Politics: Democracy After Dictatorship*, Polity, 2008, p. 32.

120 inflation began to go down: On these early years of the PSOE, see Paul Kennedy, "Spain: Exhaustion of the Left Project," *Parliamentary Affairs*, 2003(56), and Sebastian Royo, *From Social Democracy to Neoliberalism*, Palgrave Macmillan, 2000.

121 "We are neither right, nor left": Dan Hancox, "Why Ernesto Laclau Is the Figurehead, *Guardian*, February 9, 2015.

120 energy of the Indignados: On the history of Podemos, see Iglesias, *New Left Review* 72; Iglesias, *Politics in a Time of Crisis: Podemos and the Future of Democracy*, Verso, 2015; Giles Tremlett, "The Podemos Revolution," *Guardian*, March 31, 2015; author interviews with Fernando Roman and Segundo Gonzalez Garcia.

121 "the principles of Groucho Marx": Tremlett, op. cit.

122 May 15 movement: Iglesias, *New Left Review*.

122 the "pink tide": On the Latin American influence on Podemos, see Becquer Seguin, "Podemos's Latin American Roots," *Jacobin*, March 27, 2015. And on Latin American populism, see Carlos se la Torre and Cynthia J. Arnson, *Latin American Populism in the Twenty-first Century*, Washington, 2013.

122 Ernesto Laclau: See Ernesto Laclau and Chantal Mouffe, *Hegemony and Socialist Strategy*, Verso, 1985; Ernesto Laclau, *On Populist Reason*, op. cit.; Íñigo Errejón and Chantal Mouffe, *Podemos: In the*

Name of the People, Lawrence & Wishart, 2016. Laclau and Mouffe were also colleagues or mentors of several prominent leaders of Syriza, including economist Yanis Varoufakis and Rena Dourou, the governor of Athens. See Dan Hancox, "Why Ernesto Laclau Is the Intellectual Figurehead for Syriza and Podemos," *Guardian*, February 9, 2015.

123 **"indebted to the work of Laclau":** Jose Ignacio Torreblanca, *Storm the Heavens*, Debate Editorial, 2015, p. 33.

123 **endorsed Laclau and Mouffe's view:** Laclau and Mouffe, op. cit.

123 **stealing democracy from the people:** Iglesias, op. cit.

123 **left and right metaphors:** Íñigo Errejón, "Que es Podemos?" *Le Monde Diplomatique*, July 2014.

124 **"their victory is easier":** Pablo Iglesias, "Spain on the Edge," *New Left Review*, May–June 2015

124 **"at the margins":** Errejón and Mouffe, op. cit.

124 **social rights, and redistribution:** "Understanding Podemos," *New Left Review*, May–June 2015.

124 **We want a welfare state:** Interview with author.

125 **recover democracy and sovereignty:** email interview with author.

125 **unifying symbol:** Writing in his role as political theorist in *New Left Review*, Iglesias described

the strategic in Laclauian terms: "The task, then, was to aggregate the new demands generated by the crisis around a mediatic leadership, capable of dichotomizing the political space." "Understanding Podemos," op. cit.

126 **"then we take Madrid":** Lauren Frayer, "Spain's New Left-wing Party," *Los Angeles Times*, May 17, 2015.

126 **from his Twitter feed:** Cas Mudde, "Podemos and the Beginning of the End," *Guardian*, December 21, 2015.

126 **"Spain is not Greece":** *Guardian*, September 9, 2015.

127 **middle-class support:** Author's interview with political scientist Ignacio Sanchez Cueno.

127 **Unidos Podemos:** http://progressivespain.com/2016/03/09/podemos-conflict-boils-over-in-madrid-pointing-to-national-dispute-over-leadership-decision-making/.

128 **"debt in the Eurozone area":** http://www.izquierda-unida.es/sites/default/files/doc/50_Pasos_Para_Gobernar_Juntos_0.pdf (author's translation with the help of Google Translate).

128 **"seals deal with communist group":** http://elpais.com/elpais/2016/05/10/inenglish/1462867217_272449.html.

128 **192-page IKEA catalogue:** http://lasonrisadeunpais.es/programa/.

180

129 **would have done "even worse":** http://www.comiendotierra.es/2016/06/27/a-la-primera-no-va-la-vencida/ and http://politica.elpais.com/politica/2016/07/01/actualidad/1467402299_031801.html

129 **"fields remain immobile":** http://politica.elpais.com/politica/ 2016/06/29/actualidad/1467185738_087126.html

CHAPTER SIX

132 **Explained Kenneth Kristensen Berth:** Interview with author.

133 **According to one newspaper poll:** Alexander Tange, "Denmark Considers Moving Migrants," *Reuters*, January 21, 2016.

133 **said Rene Offersen:** Interview with author.

134 **murders and rapes perpetrated by recent migrants:** Alison Smale, "Migrant Crimes," *The New York Times*, May 21, 2016.

134 **nine of ten cities:** http://www.bbc.com/news/world-europe-36362505.

135 **male white working class:** Robert Ford and Matthew Goodwin, *Revolt on the Right: Explaining Support for the Radical Right in Britain*, Routledge, 2014. Also Ford and Goodwin, "Understanding UKIP," *The Political Quarterly*, September–October 2014.

136 **over 600,000 a year:** http://www.bbc.com/news/uk-politics-35658731

136 **"push British workers out of jobs":** Ibid.

145 **"native employment rates":** https://www.gov.uk/government/uploads/system/uploads/attachment_data/file/257235/analysis-of-the-impacts.pdf.

139 **less than $45,000:** http://www.newstatesman.com/politics/staggers/2016/06/how-did-different-demographic-groups-vote-eu-referendum.

142 **"world without pity":** Marine Le Pen, *À Contre Flots*, Editions Jacques Grancher, 2006, author's translations. For Marine Le Pen's life, see Elizabeth Zerofsky, "Front Runner," *Harpers*, May 2016; and Stefan Simons, "Le Pen's Daughter," *Der Spiegel*, August 2006.

141 **"reinforced the caricature":** Le Pen, op. cit., p. 256.

143 **she broke publicly with him:** "Chambres a Gas, Le Pen Persiste," *Le Figaro,* March 24, 2008. The magazine was *Bretons.*

143 **critical of Gollnisch's comments:** "Marine Le Pen Reprend ses Distances avec son Pere," *Figaro*, April 24, 2008.

143 **"party like the others:** Alexandre Deze, *Le Front national: à la conquête du pouvoir?*, Armand Colin, 2012.

143 **racists were not welcome in the party:** Mathieu von Rohr, "Marine Le Pen's Populism for the Masses," *Der Spiegel*, July 7, 2011.

144 **"by all necessary means":** http://www.bbc.com/news/world-europe-13206056

144 **finally expelling him:** http://www.bbc.com/news/world-europe-34009901

144 **"among unassimilated children?":** http://lelab.europe1.fr/debile-ou-degoutant-1403 (author's translation).

144 **she explained to an interviewer:** Russell Shorto, "Is This the Most Dangerous Woman in Europe," *The Observer*, June 26, 2011.

145 **Philippot told Le Monde:** "Florian Philippot," *Le Monde*, November 1, 2012 (author's translation).

146 **referendum held on the Euro:** http://www.frontnational.com/pdf/Programme.pdf (author's translation).

146 **Le Pen's election brochure:** http://www.frontnational.com/pdf/projet_mlp2012.pdf.

147 **and Parisians:** Nonna Mayer, "La Plafond de Verre Electoral Entame, mais pas Brise," *Les Faux-Semblants du Front National*, Presses de Sciences Po, 2015, p. 309.

147 **"Merkozy":** "Hollande contre Merkozy," *Le Monde*, June 2, 2012.

147 **abandoned his promises:** On Hollande's fall and the FN's rise, see Arthur Goldhammer, "As EU Technocrats Falter, the French Right Gains," *Boston Review*, December 16, 2015.

149 **"reached very high levels":** Pascal Perrineau, "Le Front National, une partie de plus en plus national," *Le Monde*, February 4, 2015.

149 **Socialist Party support:** Perrineau, op. cit.

150 **"other public facilities":** Interview with author.

150 **Bouvet said:** Interview with author.

150 **Frédéric Martel:** Interview with author.

151 **Zemmour explained:** Interview with author.

151 **Sébastien Chenu:** Interview with author.

152 **Antoine Golliot:** Interview with author.

152 **"gay lobby":** Sophie Pedder, "Ma rine Le Pen, L'Etrangere," *Economist 1843*, April–May 2016.

152 **buy it with francs or euros:** Olivier Faye, "Au FN, le Sujet de l'identite," *Le Monde*, June 10, 2016, author's translation.

152 **"Christians must stand up to resist Islam":** *Briebart News*, July 26, 2016.

153 **Bouvet says:** Interview with author.

CONCLUSION

154 **"Donald Trump: American Fascist":** http://billmoyers.com/story/trump-the-american-fascist/.

182   154   **"Yes, Donald Trump is a fascist":** Jamil Smith, *New Republic*, November 2015.

154   **"a fascist, extremist party":** http://www.reuters.com/article/us-eu-elections-fascism-idUSKB-N0E71ZS20140527

154   **"fascist movement":** https://www.rnw.org/archive/wilders-fascist.

154   **"Italy's New Mussolini":** http://www.spectator.co.uk/2013/03/italys-new-duce/.

156   **Kenneth Kristiansen Berth explained:** Interview with author.

156   **movements are nationalist:** See George Friedman, "Nationalism is Rising, not Fascism," May 31, 2016. https://geopoliticalfutures.com/nationalism-is-rising-not-fascism/.

158   **China's imports:** David H. Autor, David Dorn, and Gordon H. Hanson, "The China Shock," Working Paper 21906, NBER, January 2016.

158   **2.4 million jobs overseas:** https://www. americanprogress .org/issues/labor/news/ 2012/07/ 09/11898/5-facts- about-overseas-outsourcing/.

159   **"How is the immigration maximum determined?":** Ha-Joon Chang, 23 *Things They Don't Tell You About Capitalism*, Bloomsbury Press, 2011, p. 5.

159   **less willing to pay taxes:** See Michael Lind, "Open Borders or High-wage Welfare State," *Salon*, May 4, 2010. See also the controversy surrounding Robert D. Putnam's paper, *"E Pluribus Unum:* Diversity and Community in the Twenty-First Century," *Scandinavian Political Studies*, Vol. 30, No. 2, in which Putnam describes, on the basis of extensive studies, how ethnic diversity is negatively correlated with solidarity.

160   **Olivier Roy has warned:** Isaac Chotiner, "The Islamization of Radicalism," *Slate*, June 22, 2016.

162   **fulfill a redistributive role:** Wynne Godley, "Maastricht and all that," *London Review of Books*, October 8, 1992.

163   **EU is destined to disintegrate:** Jan Zielonka, *Is the EU Doomed?* Polity, 2014.

Columbia Global Reports is a publishing imprint from Columbia University that commissions authors to do original on-site reporting around the globe on a wide range of issues. The resulting novella-length books offer new ways to look at and understand the world that can be read in a few hours. Most readers are curious and busy. Our books are for them.

globalreports.columbia.edu